THE DRoPuUI
MULTI-MILLIONAIRE

37 BUSINESS LESSONS
ON HOW TO SUCCEED IN BUSINESS WITH
NO MONEY, NO EDUCATION AND NO CLUE

THE DROPOUT
MULTI-MILLIONAIRE

37 BUSINESS LESSONS
ON HOW TO SUCCEED IN BUSINESS WITH
NO MONEY, NO EDUCATION AND NO CLUE

BY BRIAN WILL

The Dropout Multi-Millionaire
37 Business Lessons on How to Succeed in Business with No Money, No Education and No Clue

ISBN: 978-1-7371538-0-1

Edited by Hilary Jastram

DEDICATION

This is the second book in a series about life and business. While the first book was a more of a personal look at my life and the things I learned growing up in less-than-ideal circumstances, this book is focused more on the things I learned when starting… growing…succeeding and failing in business over the last thirty-five years. The lessons here did not come from college or from any kind of formal education or training. They came from the street. This is a "35-year overnight success" story that can hopefully help you avoid a lot of the mistakes I made along the way.

This book is dedicated to every single person who believed in me along this journey of business and life. They served as inspiration to keep me going.

It is also dedicated to every person who didn't believe in me and who told me I would never make it. They were the fuel I needed—if only to prove them wrong—to create the burning desire to overcome all my deficiencies and push me past what I thought I couldn't do.

Finally, this book is dedicated to my business partner Steve. He taught me how to be a better person, business owner, CEO, and entrepreneur.

TABLE OF CONTENTS

TABLE OF CONTENTS

FOREWORD

I met Brian in 2001 when he was renting a portion of one of my buildings. His business was struggling back then, but he was always optimistic and persistent. I admired that about him.

He has the same philosophy that I do, which is, "You don't lose until you quit." When I saw that in him, despite his circumstances, it endeared him to me — like him, I had also started from scratch.

Over the course of that first year, our interactions grew from being business neighbors to me, becoming interested in his business.

Then my circumstances changed. After splitting off from some of my partners, the time was right to work with Brian. In 2003, Brian, one of my partners from my first companies, and I started another company together, called Monetizeit, that you will read about in this book. It was during the building phase of this business that I saw what Brian was really all about and how he operated. It was a time of learning.

Three years later, in 2006, when we sold Monetizeit, we all made a pot of money.

This was a very defining moment for us, including me. There are certain things in life that will tell you everything you need to know about somebody: One of the biggest things is what they do when hit with a windfall of money.

When we sold our company, I observed how crazy people went with the profits. A couple of our partners blew it, and several, including Brian and I, were frugal with our share. Unlike a lot of people who make money fast, you could see that Brian was appreciative and was going to use it to benefit his and his family's lives. I remember the Monday after we actually got the money, there were several new sportscars in the parking lot, but none of them were Brian's. That was a sign of good character to me.

It was such a weird time to be alive; so many 20-somethings getting rich for almost nothing. The problem was they had never put in their time in the corporate or business world. Suddenly, here they were, cashing in on whatever business opportunity paid off for them. Last year they had been average Joe's, then all of a sudden, they thought they were geniuses. But that was not Brian; he didn't lose his bearings and wasn't going to squander his chance to build off his windfall profits. He even invested them into a new industry.

In my life, I have learned that money is time. It's not things. I liked what I saw in how Brian stepped up to manage his money. We were friends by then and remain that way today, and it has everything to do with his values.

After the big sale, I went my way, and Brian went on to several other ventures, including owning restaurants. That's another thing I love about the guy; he's not afraid to take a pretty big risk. Brian will tell you that he had never owned a restaurant before, and his favorite dinner is whatever is on the take-out menu. His risks were magnified!

I was in restaurants back in my twenties, and I was really good at running one store, but I couldn't get a second location off the ground. So, I respect Brian for continuing to do what he does.

Especially because, as he explains, he makes sure not to set foot in his restaurant if he can help it. His systems are all in place to watch his staff, customers, kitchen, and everything else, and he manages it all from his phone or laptop. I couldn't do that. I'm a hands-on guy. But he's making use of technology and has an innate understanding of how to operate the business. He takes what's in existence, what people are using for systems and processes, and makes it better. Then he goes on to teach people how to save time, money, and energy, too.

He's just wired that way.

Maybe he even inspired me to throw my hat in the ring and try something new after my retirement. When I found that volunteering didn't stoke my drive, I bought a retail business. Now I've never been in retail in my life, but I'm still chugging along just like he is.

At the end of the day, you have to believe what you're doing is right. It's why I live by the motto: "As long as you do the best you can do, you don't have to worry about the outcome." You can't change it anyway. As long as I have known Brian, he has always tried his best.

As you read this book, I want you to keep in mind that you control the game. If you don't want it to be over, if you want to keep trying, live by the words: "It's not over 'til you quit."

Finally, don't deny the opportunities that might be right in front of you. Business owners and bosses are always on the hunt for good people. When you keep going, and you work in integrity, you land on their radar. That's how Brian got on mine. I saw his traits; I saw how he worked, and it was very valuable to me.

It paid off in a way that neither of us will ever forget: the year we sold our business for $60 million.

In my mind, there are sixty million reasons not to miss the opportunity to be picked out of the crowd. But what I gained was worth more than money. We are lifelong friends.

I urge you to take what Brian is sharing here seriously. He has created a whole new life for himself and his family based on his instincts and ability to stick with it. You can learn from his adventures and create new opportunities for your life that will pay off, too.

Enjoy the book, and whatever you do, don't quit.

Steve Wadley
~Friend

PREFACE

Let's start with a little background. "This book is about failure."

I actually love this opening line because it sets the tone for everything you're about to read … and hopefully learn. I really want to drive that point home…because if you don't understand that success is born of failure, then you should stop reading now and come back later when you're ready to accept that fundamental truth.

Yes, this book is about failure. It's also about success.

The underlying principle is that you cannot succeed at a high level unless you have first failed ... And then learned ... and I failed a lot.

In the last thirty-five years, I have founded or co-founded six different, very successful companies in four different industries. I franchised a landscaping company, have done three startups in the insurance industry, as well as an internet marketing company, and I now own a chain of restaurants. Two of my companies were sold to venture capital firms, and one went to a private equity firm. One of those companies went public. At their peak, the successful companies I built and sold were worth hundreds of millions of dollars. I have also consulted for multiple companies, from small businesses to multi-billion-dollar private and public companies in the areas of sales and management. I became a millionaire at the age of forty and made over a million dollars a year for the first time at the age of forty-one.

I also started many other companies that weren't successful at all. Many of them failed spectacularly, and I lost a significant amount of money. I would go so far as to say, I have failed far more than I've succeeded.

What I want you to understand is, while I failed, I also learned. That is why I love the phrase... "Sometimes you win ... sometimes you learn." Failing is the key to success!

What kind of filter do you have?

Learning through failure is one of the most powerful experiences you can have. Applying your lessons gleaned through failure is what will make you successful in the future. Learning through failure is how you develop your "success filter."

Every one of us has a subconscious filter that we use to instantly analyze virtually every decision we make. Everything you see and hear goes through this filter before your brain accepts it or rejects it. Chances are, you don't even realize you have this filter, and you have probably never thought about the fact that it is controlling every decision you have ever made.

This filter operates on a subconscious level. You literally don't even know it's happening ... and it's happening in real-time. It is the sum total of every single experience you have ever had. It is a product of your interactions with each person you have allowed to be a part of your life. It is the entirety of every written word of every book you have ever read and everything you have ever seen on TV or elsewhere.

Your brain has learned from everything it has ever been exposed to.

Whatever and whoever you allowed access to put information into your brain has helped to form this filter.

This subconscious learning is similar to that of a child who has grown up in France, speaking French and not English. Their brain has been exposed to French, and so, that is how they think. They will always think and speak French. Their mannerisms will be French. They will judge the world around them based on growing up in France. They will always think this way unless, at some point, they decide to learn something else.

Only then will they start to see life from a different perspective. They can allow themselves to learn a new language. They can experience different world views. The only challenge with this new change is that they will be filtering all this new information through their current "French Based" filter that they have developed their entire life. The current filter will then either accept the new information or reject it. This process of change will take time and effort and will not be easy.

Now think of all the people in your life and all the media you absorb every day.

Your absorption of the world around you started the day you were born. Your parents started putting information into your brain from day one during what is called the nurturing phase of life. You will always be a product of whatever information they put in there.

Here is where it gets interesting and complicated. The information they put into your brain was a product of *their parents* and *their lives* growing up.

You are literally the next step in the evolution of your family learning.

Then you went to school, and your teachers started influencing you. They pushed you in new directions and new ways of thinking. What they taught you came from *their parents* and *their educational background*. Many times, this information conflicted with what your parents had taught you, so your brain had to start making decisions on what to think and believe. Your filter and the way you saw the world was challenged.

Then there were your friends. They also had different thoughts about the world from *their parents* and *their upbringing*. They tried to influence you to think their way. We call this peer pressure. Once again, your brain had to decide what to accept and what to reject. Your choice of friends is important on many levels. Your filter continued to evolve.

This process of new input continued through high school and maybe college, where your professors got their shot at changing the way you think. They also wanted to affect your personal filter to think their way, based on *their life experiences ... their education ... their friends,* and *their parents*.

Even today, your decision-making process is affected by everything around you in life. In fact, your filter can instantly change based on the last argument you had with your spouse or the last book you read … or even this book you are reading right now. You will accept or reject what is in here based on that filter.

Every future decision you make will be filtered based on whatever experiences you have had in the past, as well as what is currently going on in your life. Your brain will then make an instant decision as to whether to accept or reject the information and whether or not you should add it to your filter to be used at a later date. All this activity is going on behind the scenes. You are probably not controlling it… No, it is controlling you, and you have no idea it's even happening.

If you think about the billions of bits of information that your mind has soaked up and the endless avenues that it took to gain everything you know … it's quite amazing. Each of us took all that information and accepted or rejected it, and then we made it part of our critical thinking process—our personal filter. We are literally a product of not just our past but of the past families and histories of everyone in our lives.

I can't stress enough how important this filter is to your life. You will succeed or fail in life and in your business endeavors because of this filter and the decisions it leads you to make.

When it comes to your career...

So here you are, brand new in your business, making decisions every day that will affect your family and your future.

Chances are you haven't been successful in your own business yet, and you don't have any experience making the kind of decisions you are going to need to make moving forward to keep yourself out of the business failure statistics listed on the back of this book's cover. Most people in this situation would start talking to friends and family about their thoughts on what to do.

If this is you, I want you to ask yourself a few questions about the people you're taking advice from:

1. Are they businesspeople?

2. Are they successful in whatever endeavor you want to pursue?

3. Do your friends have the successful experience and knowledge you need to influence your decision-making as you grow a business?

These are critical questions you need to ask yourself before you accept advice from anyone, and especially from anyone you personally know.

This next sentence is so important that I am going to highlight it…. **If you … or whoever you took advice from … has never experienced real success in what you are trying to achieve, you will not have the correct filter or the critical thinking skills** needed to make the right decisions when they must be made. **You will only guess at the path you should take.**

If by chance, you get lucky and make the right decision, that will go into your filter, and it will help you make more good decisions down the road. But if you make the wrong decisions **and don't learn from them**, your filter will become a negative *"failure magnet."* That negative filter will set you on a path of continuously making bad decisions. You will technically be conditioning your mind to fail ... and once that happens, you will be hard-pressed to change it on your own. You will need help from someone who can show you how to make better decisions and succeed.

A very successful and wealthy friend once told me, **the only difference between a rich and successful person and a broke person ... is the way they think.**

Let me say that again ...

The only difference between you ... and Bill Gates, or Jeff Bezos ... or Elon Musk ... is the way you think...

That's it.

They started life the same way you did. But they went on to be wildly successful because of how they think and what they have in their filter—what they have exposed themselves to and learned.

Do you have a success filter or a failure filter? The good news is you can change it if you want to—as long as you're willing to listen and learn from someone who has the success you want. Then you just have to take the time and effort to do it.

There are two business lessons that I want you to retain as you move on from this section of the book.

Business Lesson #1... *Be careful what you allow in your brain. It will affect everything in your life.*

Business Lesson #2... *Be honest about your situation and your personal filter. If you do not have a success filter, you need to find someone who does and allow them to help you. The only thing standing between you and success in this situation is your ego. Your ego will take you down a dark path if you let it. The truly unfortunate part here is **that if you do not have a success filter, you will probably not make the right decision to allow someone to help you**, and your failure filter will continue to evolve just like it has in the past.*

The old saying, "The rich get richer, and the poor get poorer," is true. It is a product of having either a success or a failure filter.

One Last Point of Order

I am always right

Let me explain.

Everything you are going to read here will work 100% of the time ... 80% of the time.

This means that 20% of the time, what I'm telling you will not work because of outlier situations that always pop up.

Outliers are certain situations that defy logic, cheat justice, or are a result of pure, undeserved luck. That said, 80% of the time,

I am right ... and since I just told you that I'm wrong 20% of the time... I'm actually right about that as well ... which makes me right ... 100% of the time!!!

So, if you disagree with me on a certain point and feel the need to tell me I'm wrong... Well, I already told you I'm wrong 20% time, which means I'm still right.

Wrap your head around that for a minute, then let's get started!

INTRODUCTION

This book started out as an afterthought to my first book, which I completed last year.

That first book took five years to write. As I was finishing the original manuscript, I felt like I wasn't done.

I was out in Park City for a month skiing and had just finished the rough draft of the first book. Afterward, I went to dinner at a local brewery. While I was sitting there, I wondered if I could actually write another book… *Do I have enough material in me to get a whole other book on paper?* I pulled out my cell phone, opened the notes section, and started dictating ideas and topics. Within thirty minutes, I had over 100 ideas on paper that I could further develop.

That got me excited, so I finished my dinner, went back to the condo, and built an outline that night.

That was six months ago, and during the writing process, I discovered an interesting truth about myself that I use to help me finish my books.

I find that I cannot write very well while I am home, so I end up doing all my writing while I am away at the beach or someplace else with no distractions. In fact, I am sitting at my place on Clearwater Beach, Florida, right now, typing this introduction.

I came in for the weekend with the specific intent of finishing this second manuscript. As I sit here and pound it out, I figure I should have it off to my editor for the first round of editing by Monday morning, just in time for me to head back to Atlanta.

INTRODUCTION

This book is the product of thirty-five years of building businesses, consulting for various companies from small to Fortune 500, and training salespeople, managers, executives, and owners of businesses.

It is crafted from a series of lessons told through actual stories I have lived through. What is contained in these pages is by no means all of the stories; there are probably a hundred more. Hopefully, I picked some good ones to help you out along the way.

I also hope you find this book both entertaining and useful as a tool to help you grow your business. I wish I had known what I am sharing here thirty-five years ago. It would have made my journey a WHOLE lot easier...

CHAPTER 1

A FEW QUESTIONS

"Successful people ask better questions, and as a result, they get better answers." –Tony Robbins

Do you consider yourself a business owner?

Do you believe you are an entrepreneur?

Not surprisingly, most people who have their own business think they are both. The reality, however, is that most people who have their own business are not.

Now that doesn't seem to make sense, I know. But it's true. So, before you get mad, put this book down and call me crazy; let's dig into this statement.

Most people who start a business "incorporate" it. They do this because they believe it will provide them personal liability protection. Protections from liability, however, come with a new set of rules that must be followed in order to take advantage of those protections. This is where most small businesspeople get tripped up.

We'll start with the definition of a corporation (your new business) to make this a little clearer.

A corporation is a legal entity that is separate and distinct from its owners. Corporations enjoy most of the rights and responsibilities that individuals possess; they can enter contracts, loan and borrow money, sue and be sued, hire employees, own assets, and pay taxes. Some refer to them as a "legal person."

Pay attention to the last line ... a corporation is essentially a separate **"legal person"** that legal person should be able to stand on its own, separate and apart from the owner of the business itself. If the owner and the business are being treated as the **"same,"** then the corporation doesn't really exist, and the business is just an extension of the owner. It's not a "business" in the technical term. It is what we call a **"self-employed" person**.

Based on this, let me ask you a few questions about your business...

1. If you stop showing up to work, if you stop going to the job site, or if you stop trying to sell your product or services, what happens to your business?

2. Do you provide most of the sales? Do you do most of the technical work?

3. If you went into a coma, would your business continue without you?

4. Do your customers rely on your personal knowledge and expertise?

5. Who can do your job if you go on vacation for six months?

6. What would happen if you turned off your cell phone and didn't check in?

If your business relies on you to get through an average day, week, or month, then your "business" is really an extension of you. It is not a separate functioning entity without you. It is not as much a business as it is a job you have created for yourself in your industry.

> **You may have a business name, you may have an office, and you might even be incorporated, but if your business is focused on you... you are self-employed.**

Business Lesson #3... *You need to start by being honest about what you have. Are you self-employed? Is that what you want? Don't fool yourself into thinking you have more than you do. You can't grow if you can't be honest with yourself.*

I want to make sure the distinction between having a business and being self-employed is clear. You need to understand this because it will be the foundation of what we are going to talk about later in the book. It relates to who you are, what you really have in terms of your business — and finally, where you want to take your business.

Understand also, being self-employed is not a bad thing. It's WAY better than having a job, in my opinion. It can create a great lifestyle, and you can make a lot of money. I just want you to know that it also has its limitations.

To elaborate: you may not have a boss, but **your personal life is still controlled by your customers,** and you still need to show up for work every day.

If you leave, your customers go away, and you are out of business.

Again, this is not a bad thing, but you need to understand what you have and decide if that is what you want ... or if you want something bigger that has value and is more secure.

You get the point.

In my case, I have never wanted to be self-employed. I have always wanted to be a business owner. More specifically, I wanted to own something that lives and breathes without needing me to manage it every day. I wanted it to stand alone and survive without me if need be and for it to be an independent entity that wasn't intertwined into my presence and personality.

Based on this idea of the difference between being self-employed and owning a business, there are certain things that I have done and still do in each business I start to make sure that I am taking the right actions to own a business vs. being self-employed.

When I start a business, I have several goals in mind.

1. **I don't want my customers to know me.** I own a small chain of restaurants right now, and I don't really ever step foot in them unless I want free food or to have drinks with my friends. My customers generally have no idea who I am, and they don't come in to see me.

As I write this, I am sitting at my beach place five hundred miles from my restaurants, and they are just fine without me. If I sold the restaurants, nobody would miss me. This is how you create value. If your goal is to one day sell your business, then you need to understand that nobody wants to **buy** a business with a customer base that only knows the owner because when the owner goes, so does the business.

2. **I don't want my employees to need me**. When I owned the online insurance agency, other people ran the company. I would come in at 11ish, go to lunch at noon, and leave at four. I would actually tell people who came into my office and asked questions, "I have no idea... I'm useless." Even if I knew the answer to the question they were asking, I refused to answer. I would force people to find the answer on their own or get the information from someone else who would figure it out for them. I absolutely refused to allow people to rely on me for anything.

Remember, nobody wants to buy a business that needs the special knowledge or skill of the owner to run it. That type of business has a LOT less value.

When I sold that company to a venture capital firm out of Silicon Valley, I left, and they replaced me with one of their people. My employees kept right on rolling along. I was irrelevant, and that has value.

3. Speaking of value and selling... **When I start a business, my goal is to sell it.** I don't know when I will do that. I don't know who I will sell it to. What I do know is that I am building something with value that I will eventually sell and make a bunch of money off of.

When my partners and I started the online marketing and lead-gen company, we went in knowing the metrics we had to hit to create the value we wanted to sell it for. We did this upfront. That was the goal from day one.

**We were acquired by a private equity firm
out of Chicago for nearly $60 million two-and-a-half
years after we opened our doors.
Yes, we hit our numbers.**

Again, there is absolutely nothing wrong with being self-employed, but I personally do not want to be Joe of "Joes Plumbing." I do not want my income or my future to rely on me. When Self-Employed Joe gets sick, or if he can't work, he doesn't make any money, the business fails, and Joe goes broke.

Business Lesson #4... *If you want to own a business and build value, don't be Joe.*

CHAPTER 2

SELF-EMPLOYED VS. BUSINESS OWNER—WHAT ARE YOU?

"A big business starts small." –Richard Branson

Let's dig a little more deeply into defining the difference between a business owner and a person who is self-employed.

As I referenced earlier, self-employed people are usually independent contractors or consultants, or they run small businesses with either only them or very few employees. They are integral to the daily operations of their company. It is their knowledge and expertise that make the business go.

Business owners, on the other hand, own a company that has value "without them." They have infrastructure. They have key employees. They have processes and procedures they do not have to manage. They are *not* the most important part of their day-to-day operations.

Most people launch their business as a self-employed person and then face the choice to either stay self-employed or grow their new venture into something much larger and more valuable.

My First Lightbulb Moment, and… One of Us is Stupid

Thirty-three years ago, in 1987, I had just gotten married and was living with my new wife in my grandmother's back bedroom. We literally moved in the day after we got married.

I didn't move there because it was a huge house and we just loved it. I moved us in there because we had no car, no jobs, and no place to live.

We were twenty-one years old and were broke and homeless with no transportation!

Shortly after moving into my grandmother's house, my best friend Max, who I met during my short stint in college, called me. He worked for a landscaping company, and they needed help.

Max wanted to know if I would be interested in coming to work with him, mowing grass, at the landscaping company. At such a young age, I was a big-time negotiator.

So, I said, "Well, Max, I am kind of busy with other projects ... and umm, I have a few irons in the fire. What exactly are you offering?" Max told me he could pay me $4 an hour, but to sweeten the deal, he would pay me cash every Friday. After considering his offer for a few seconds, I questioned, "Cash?" He affirmed that was the case, and I accepted his offer. The next day I was out at 7 am working with Max and our supervisor, Sam, mowing lawns.

This was my first job after getting married, and unbeknownst to me at the time, it would launch my career in business.

Each day the drill was the same, Max, Sam, and I would drive to someone's house and get out and mow their grass. When we were done, Sam would go up to the door and collect a check. He would then come back to the truck and write in a notebook the name of the client and the check amount.

After about two weeks of this, I was sitting in the truck one day when I opened the notebook to see what was in there. It turned out we were mowing about eighty lawns a week at an average price of $25. We were pulling in $2000 a week. I was amazed at the breakdown; I was getting paid about $160 a week. Max was making $200 a week, and Sam was making about $400 a week. That added up to $760. Throw in some fuel costs and miscellaneous expenses, and the overhead on our crew was about $1000 a week.

At the end of each day, we would drive over to Tim's house. Tim owned the company, and we were ONE of his crews. We would pull up to the front of the house; Sam would get out of the truck, walk up to the front door and hand Tim the money for the day. We would then leave to put the equipment away and go home, only to return the next day to do it again.

The business model of this landscaping company wouldn't leave my mind. I couldn't stop thinking about the work I was doing and what I was getting paid versus the owner.

One random day of the week, sitting in the truck in front of someone's house, all sweaty from working outside in the summer heat, I looked at that notebook and thought to myself, *after our $1000 in expenses, Tim is still making $1000 a week net, just from our crew and he has four crews working, while I'm out here doing all the work making $160!!*

Now I was not the smartest person...

I don't have a college education.

And let's be honest, I was working a $4 an hour job...but come on, man, I could cut grass!

That's when the proverbial lightbulb went off in my head. It suddenly dawned on me, sitting there in the truck, that ... **ONE OF US IS STUPID** ... and I knew which one of us it was!!!

I'm probably not supposed to use the word stupid; I could have said one of us is smarter, but remember, I was twenty-one. Those were my exact thoughts.

Two weeks after starting work with Max and Sam, I quit my job and started my first business. It was called Diamond Lawn Scape.

I tell you this story because this exact same scenario plays out all over the country every day.

This is how most businesses start.

They are started by regular people working for someone else, who usually work as a key employee at another company. One day they do the same thing I did. Likely they were just sitting at work when they said to themselves, *why am I working for these jokers? I do all the work, and they get all the money. I can make more money if I do this on my own.*

Five hundred thousand new businesses start every month in America…This is how it usually begins… every single day.

Here's the catch…

Unfortunately, these people also usually think that starting and operating their own business will be easy and that anybody can do it.

I fell into this category myself that day I sat in the truck and leafed through that notebook. I **didn't have a clue** what I was doing. I just figured it was easy since I had seen others do it, so I jumped in headfirst.

Another two weeks later, I had my own business. At least, that is what I thought; in reality, I was just self-employed. *Key question … Do you see the difference based on what you've learned so far?*

As part of my new lawn mowing business, I had to go out and get new customers. I was in charge of running the mower and the weed eater while my wife followed behind me with the blower to clean up the grass. We were a team. We didn't have any employees, and If I was sick and didn't go cut the grass, I would not make any money. Our business had no value without me. I was Self-Employed Joe…

Tim, my former boss, on the other hand, had a business. He owned an actual company and had multiple crews out working every day for him. When I quit working for his company, he didn't miss me. Some new guy was on my old crew the next day. His supervisors were out meeting with customers and generating new sales. If one person was out, he could move another person into the slot and keep going. If Tim went on vacation, Sam would still cut the grass and pick up the checks. When Tim got back from vacation, he would have a mountain of checks sitting there. The business did not rely on Tim being out there doing the work. Tim's business had value.

I may have been Joe when I started. But I wanted to be Tim.

That day would come, but it wouldn't be for a long time. I still had a LOT to learn.

Business Lesson #5... *Decide what you want to be: self-employed or a business owner. Making that decision is the first step toward how you are going to structure your company moving forward and build your future.*

CHAPTER 3

OK, YOU'RE IN BUSINESS —NOW, WHO ARE YOU?

"Only those who risk going too far can possibly find out how far one can go." –T.S. Eliot

OK, let's assume you either have or you want to build a business, maybe a BIG business. You want to create value, and maybe, just maybe, one day, you might want to sell it and do something different or sail off into the sunset.

Every successful business is built around a team. That team should consist of different personalities. I believe there are four distinct personalities that are needed for success:

1. the Entrepreneur,

2. the Manager,

3. the Salesperson,

4. and the Specialist.

These personalities fill different roles in the organizations, and each of these roles **should** enhance each other. Where you are weak, you need to hire someone who is strong. Where you get bogged down in details, you need to hire someone to handle the minutia, so you can focus on the big picture. This seems like a pretty simple concept. **But the problem** with this concept, or the execution of it, **usually comes down to the owner.**

People who start businesses have a common problem. They think they have the answer to everything and that everything they think is right. They believe that because they started the venture, they must have all the answers.

You might've guessed: they have egos.

Most people who start businesses also tend to believe that they are both entrepreneurs and managers, when most of the time, they are actually salespeople or specialists. We will discuss the reason behind this shortly but for the moment, just remember that not knowing what role you play in an organization is the first sign of trouble and the beginning of the end.

Before we go any further, let's define the four key types of people in the organization so we can understand who they are — but more importantly, who *you* are.

Entrepreneurs

Everyone who starts a business is not an entrepreneur. I know you hear the term "entrepreneur" thrown around a lot, but it's usually thrown around by someone who doesn't understand what they are talking about. It's an ego word. It's sexy. Everyone wants to be an entrepreneur.

For those of you who are now going to go google the definition of an entrepreneur … let me save you some time.

The Oxford Language definition reads like this:

"A person who organizes and operates a business or businesses, taking on greater than normal financial risks in order to do so."

On the surface, that seems pretty straightforward. Simply looking at it means anyone who starts a business is an entrepreneur. The challenge here is twofold.

First ... it says a "business." We have already discussed the technical differences between a "business" and being self-employed. It's a technicality but is worth noting. It doesn't say someone who takes on being self-employed.

Second ... it says, "takes on and operates." By that definition, a failed business is also a failed entrepreneur. Or more correctly, a failed business is someone who thought they were an entrepreneur but really weren't. There is a big difference between being an entrepreneur and being a failed business owner.

The challenge here is the conflict between a "perceived" entrepreneur and a "real" entrepreneur. The conflict lies in the understanding of what an entrepreneur really is ... It's not just starting a business. It's a mindset. It's a skillset. It's someone with the correct kind of personal success filter who is able to make the right decisions to successfully operate a business.

Traits of an entrepreneur:

- They think at thirty-thousand feet.
- They see the future.
- They are conceptual in nature and are generally terrible at details.

- Don't ask them to sit too long in a meeting or tolerate someone who can't think as fast as they do.

- Most of the time, they don't understand the details and don't want to.

- They think in bullet points

- They are great for bouncing ideas off of, as long as they don't have to execute them.

- They are risk-takers.

- They think in visions and abstract.

- They have a creative and future-thinking filter and can usually manage a lot of tasks at a very high level but have a hard time handling a single task from beginning to end.

- They manage chaos.

I am well-known in all the companies I have been involved with for the following phrase: "Something is wrong. I don't know what, but I'm telling you, something is wrong."

This phrase usually comes after looking at our weekly or monthly P&Ls (by the way, you can run a company completely with a good set of P&Ls and built-in metrics, but that is another chapter), or after a conversation with one of the managers, or customers.

I can feel there is a problem before any proof of it can be seen. I can't put my finger on it, but I know it's there. When I feel this way, I usually tell whoever is in charge of that area to start figuring it out. Their response might be, "Well, what is it?" To which

I answer, "I don't know. I'm just telling you there is a problem in this area. Start analyzing everything until you find it."

Eighty percent of the time, that person will come back with: "You were right. Here is the problem, and we are fixing it."

Katy, who runs my restaurant chain, calls me *the rain man*... I can see potential and future problems that are not currently visible. This is a common trait of an entrepreneur.

Here is the secret about the entrepreneur. They are probably the most important and the least important person in the organization.

You need them, but they cannot make much happen without the team. Most entrepreneurs eventually get replaced by a real CEO as the company grows beyond the entrepreneur's ability to run it.

The new CEO becomes the company manager. Then the entrepreneur either sells out or ends up on the board of directors as a thought leader and will not be as involved in the actual execution of the business.

In every company I've sold, I was replaced as the CEO, and the company grew to the next level. Entrepreneurs need the excitement of the next thing. Managing the current thing is too boring to them.

Managers

Managers are the backbone of the organization. They are in charge of the details that must be handled to run a company. They post schedules and take care of hiring and firing paperwork. They deal with the employees and manage the facilities. Managers tend to be singularly focused individuals. They are amazing at executing the task they are given but generally don't see past that to the bigger picture. Most managers likely have a degree and got good grades in college. They build processes and procedures around the vision they are given. They understand the insurance and unemployment paperwork. Managers handle the filing and phone systems. They understand the vendor payment schedules and how to upgrade QuickBooks so more than one person can look at it at a time. They know when the sales taxes are due and how to log into the state tax portal to pay it online. They know where the required posters need to hang to be in compliance with labor laws. They build the employee manual and know the forms you need to fill out and submit, so you won't get sued for sexual harassment.

Managers generally don't like change. Change requires new processes and procedures, and they've already implemented and trained the employees on the old way of doing things and don't want to have to do it all over again.

In a fast-moving, changing environment, managers tend to get frustrated. They are good at communication with the team and generally make the operation run as smoothly as possible. Mangers are critical because they handle the details the entrepreneur can't and won't. Without a manager, the company is a mess and eventually falls apart. If you don't have a manager in your company, or if you think you're a manager and you're not, you're in big trouble.

Entrepreneurs usually start out as managers in their new companies, even though that's not their strong point. Getting your business off the ground and through its initial growth phase is more about vision than process — and remember, this is where the entrepreneur shines. However, once things are rolling, the company needs a good manager to take over these tasks before the wheels come off the bus.

Salesperson

Salespeople are gunslingers. They are cowboys. They think fast, talk fast, and make things happen. They are the lifeblood of an organization. They drive sales and generate revenue … and revenue makes the world go around. Without salespeople, you don't have a company. Salespeople also push limits. They will walk out to the bleeding edge of right and wrong and hang one foot over the cliff of doom to get a deal done. Salespeople are storytellers. They are fun. They don't lie, but they know how to bend the truth to fit their narrative. Black and white become all gray. They can take a client out, wine, and dine them and make them laugh all night long.

Salespeople are generally high-strung. They have big egos and live by the motto, "You eat what you kill." They love the thrill of the hunt and signing a deal. It's fun for them.

Salespeople are in the income column of the business, unlike managers and entrepreneurs who are in the expense column. (I will explain what I mean by putting managers and entrepreneurs in the "expense column" in a later chapter of this book.) For now, just remember that salespeople are in the income column of the P&L.

Entrepreneurs can also be salespeople. The thirty-thousand-foot view fits into a sales pitch very easily.

Back in 1999, I sold my first online insurance agency. The dot-com world was just starting to crank along. Ideas were gold back then. I sold my insurance call center to a venture capital firm in Atlanta. We were absorbed by one of their portfolio companies, and then I went to work at their office in the Georgia Tech Development center. A few months in, Mitch (who was the CTO) and I came up with an idea to take our online direct-to-consumer-sales platform and turn it into a SaaS (Sales as a Service) company. (Yeah, I didn't know what that stood for at the time, either.)

We would sell the technology and an insurance quoting system directly to the insurance carriers instead of selling individual policies directly to the consumer. It was a genius idea if I do say so myself!! Now today, there are lots of companies doing this, but in the year 2000, it had not been done yet, and we figured we could generate millions in reoccurring revenue to the company.

So, we developed a business plan and a pricing structure and started calling insurance carriers to see if they would be interested in this type of software service. Within the first week, we had interest and set up a few appointments to go pitch our new *"currently-undeveloped-although-they-didn't-know-this-at-the-time"* software platform.

Please understand that I had NO experience in software sales and absolutely **no clue** how any of the technology worked. I had never pitched anything to CEOs and CTOs of billion-dollar companies. The closest I'd ever gotten to a board room was the front door on the building!

What I had was a **vision** and a few buzz words...

I had a PowerPoint presentation that we had built together ... and I had Mitch, our CTO, who was the smartest guy in the room, sitting beside me.

A week later, we rolled into our first presentation, and I went to work. I was a salesperson. That's what I did. During my pitch, I would filter in a few technical buzzwords Mitch had taught me on the plane ride there to keep the CTO interested. Then I would throw out financial projections and ROI numbers for the finance guys and CEO.

When I finished talking, it was time for questions. I could handle the basics. It was software at its core, but it was still just a sales system, and I knew sales. Mitch would sit there quietly with his master's degree in computer engineering from an Ivy League school. If a technical question came up, I wouldn't say a word; I would just look over at Mitch. That was his cue to talk. He could wow them with technical stuff. While he did that, I nodded my head like I had a clue what he was saying. When he was done, I would look back at the room for the next question.

**These people had absolutely no idea ...
that I had no idea ... what I was talking about.**

I had **NO education**. I graduated high school after almost getting kicked out with a 1.2-grade point average, and I dropped out of college. Three years earlier, I'd been mowing people's grass as a landscaper.

Before that, I'd lived with my grandmother because I had quit my job as a busboy at Applebee's to get married.

But there I was selling million-dollar insurance software packages. It was awesome.

Mitch and I perfected our dance and sold over $6 million worth of software in our first three months. I was an entrepreneur and salesperson. Mitch was the technician, and we had a whole team back at the office managing deals after we set them up. As a side note, that company changed its entire business model after our initial success and ended up going public a few years later.

Specialists

Specialists are the workhorses of companies.

To understand how specialists fit in, you need to understand the process of building a company. First, we have an idea. Then we build a company around it. Then we have a salesperson sell our product or service to someone. Once it's sold, our specialist has to perform the work. This is where Joe (from our plumber example) comes back in. Joe is out there day in and day out doing the physical work of the company. Again, without Joe, our specialist, we don't have a business, and we don't make any money. Joe is critical. Joe is in the income column. In many small businesses, Joe is also the owner (self-employed), which is the core issue with Joe's inability to grow and scale.

Who Are You?

OK, so now we know the people we need in our business. I'm betting as you read about the four types of people that you identified yourself as one or two of those. If you did, great. If you thought you were more than two, however, you're wrong. These are distinct personalities and generally don't go together.

Instead of getting bogged down with overthinking the different tasks and what you do, I want you to focus on **who you are**. You may be forced to play more than two roles initially, but you will never grow your business trying to do the things you are not good at. You will always be self-employed.

> **The problem with being unable to scale starts when a budding young new business owner thinks he or she can be all four personalities.**

What's worse is when I hear someone say, "Well, I'm just faster than everyone else, so it's easier for me to do it myself." When I hear that, it's a sign of a much larger pending issue. If you **want** to remain self-employed, you can probably keep doing everything yourself, but you will not build a big business, and you will probably never sell it. Meaning you will always be small, or your personal workload will become so big that it will burn you out—or both. Your chance of failure is very high.

Fifty percent of businesses fail in the first year. To succeed big, you need to focus on who you are. Focus on your strengths and bring in someone else to handle everything else.

I have found that entrepreneurs and salespeople can be the same person initially. They can sell the dream. Although to grow and create value, you eventually need to break them up. I have also found that entrepreneurs are generally terrible managers and specialists. They just aren't detail-oriented enough to handle the everyday details.

Salespeople also don't usually make good managers; it's too slow of a pace for them, and operational details get skipped in the name of efficiency.

Managers do not make good salespeople because the sales process is too fluid, and it changes by the minute. As we discussed, managers don't like change.

When you first throw open your doors, you may have to fill all the roles, but you will need to backfill them with the right people as quickly as possible if you're going to grow. We will explore this a bit in the next chapter.

Business Lesson #6... *Figure out who you are at your core. Don't focus on the tasks you are performing now. Don't let your ego fool you into thinking you are something that you are not. You have to be brutally honest, or your growth will stagnate.*

CHAPTER 4

TWO EXAMPLES OF SPECIALISTS WHO THINK THEY ARE ENTREPRENEURS

"Specialists can never practice their specialties too much. The danger is in not practicing enough. Make that mistake, and soon you may not be in the specialty business anymore." –Johnny Unitas

Most people who I have seen start businesses and struggle are either specialists or salespeople. Both of these people have a unique set of problems as it relates to successfully managing or growing a business. Let's start with the specialists.

1. Joe doesn't have a clue.

In an earlier chapter, we talked about Self-Employed Joe. Joe was the key employee at a plumbing company. (This can be any type of small company.) He was the guy who went out every day and did all the work. As far as Joe was concerned, he was the guy who generated revenue in the company but only got a fraction of it in his salary. His company charged $125 an hour for Joe's time and paid him $40 an hour. Joe saw this and thought his company was making more than him. He even thought that he did all the work. Joe liked to tell his friends, "That's not right... Without me, they have nothing!!!" So, one day Joe got out of bed and said, I'm going to start Joe's Plumbing Company and make all the money myself." Joe's new business is born. He thinks he is a business owner and an entrepreneur.

Unfortunately for Joe, he doesn't understand all the work that goes on behind the scenes. He starts his business and gets a few jobs but doesn't know how to set up any type of accounting software, and he doesn't track expenses. Joe just goes to work, finishes a job, and deposits his checks.

Joe starts an LLC. He thinks he has personal protection from lawsuits. But he has no idea what the term "piercing the corporate veil" means.

(This is the definition according to the Cornell Law Legal Information Institute: "'Piercing the corporate veil' refers to a situation in which courts put aside limited liability and hold a corporation's shareholders or directors personally liable for the corporation's actions or debts. Veil piercing is most common in close corporations."[1])

He may fail to hold his annual manager's meeting and maintain the proper documentation. Joe also occasionally co-mingles his business funds with personal funds. (meaning he deposits company money into his personal account or pays personal bills with company money).

He figures it's all his money anyway, so it doesn't matter.

---

[1]

https://www.law.cornell.edu/wex/piercing_the_corporate_veil#:~:text=%22Piercing%20the%20corporate%20veil%22%20refers,most%20common%20in%20close%20corporations.

Joe doesn't understand that co-mingling funds take away all the legal protection.

Remember, a corporation is a separate entity (a legal person). Legally you can't just take someone else's money… Just like you can't go to your neighbor's mailbox and take their paycheck and deposit it in your account or buy something for yourself with your neighbor's credit card. That is illegal. In the eyes of the court system, if you do these things with company money, then the company isn't real. The company is really just you, and your personal protection is gone.

Joe also doesn't know all the different types of insurance he needs. He hires a guy or two to work for him but doesn't know how to set up his employee withholding accounts, so he just pays his crew as subcontractors and issues checks to them on Fridays. Joe also didn't get workman's comp insurance because he mistakenly thought if he paid his people as subcontractors, he didn't need to. Joe has a date with destiny at this point; he just doesn't know it yet.

Joe is good at what he does, so he continues to get work. He makes some money but soon realizes that if he is working, he is not selling new jobs. So, Joe ends up with a lot of downtime while he tries to work and sell.

When Joe completes a project, he pays his guys and deposits the rest of the money in his account. He thinks he is making a big profit. If the stars all align, Joe will go on like this for a while. Until…

The day one of Joe's guys gets hurt on the job. Joe sends him home and thinks since he is a subcontractor, he has no liability. This guy now goes home and sees a commercial on TV from some ambulance-chaser attorney. The next thing you know, Joe is in trouble and getting sued.

He is also illegally paying his employees as subcontractors when the law states that they are supposed to be W2 employees. Now the state is getting involved, and Joe has a new problem because he was not paying the appropriate withholding taxes.

Since Joe was also not carrying the proper required insurance, he's now getting sued by his employee and the state — that has filed a case against him as well.

Remember, Joe thinks he is an LLC, and he can't get sued personally. The lawyer for his former employee, the "subcontractor," however, requests all of Joe's personal and business records. The lawyer finds holes that take away Joe's protection. Joe has forgotten to pay his annual fee to the state, or he took money out of the company account without properly accounting for it. Maybe Joe used a little money to buy something personal and wrote it off to the company. Well, if Joe did that, he committed tax fraud.

The lawyer pierces the veil of Joe's LLC, and Joe goes down. He has to file bankruptcy. His business is gone, and Joe blames everyone, and everything else for his failure, when the problem was Joe just didn't understand what he was doing.

Joe was not a businessperson. He was a specialist, and he didn't listen to his friends who are business owners. They warned Joe that he needed to do all these things to protect himself. Joe either thought what they were talking about was never going to happen to him or that doing everything and getting the protection he needed was just not worth the money he would have to pay.

For the record, everything I have told you about in the previous paragraphs has happened to me, or I have had friends whose businesses failed because of these same issues. These are not things I made up... These are real-world experiences that happened to me. I had to learn about them the hard way. Now, I hope you can learn from me and not some lawyer or judge.

These are just a few of the things that can trip Joe up and what Joe doesn't understand when he is out in the field as a specialist. The complication here is that Joe is not a business owner; he is also not a manager, but he didn't know that ... and that is why he failed.

Don't be Joe.

Business Lesson #7... *Get your house in order. There are a lot of things you need to have in place to protect you and your business before you begin. If you don't know what they are, find someone who does know. The two biggest protections to put in place and where you need to be informed are having the right insurance and understanding the government regulations around your business and employees. Do not skip these, and don't ever mess with government regulations. You cannot win against them. Ever.*

2. Joe's filter will not allow him to listen.

This is probably the single biggest hindrance to most small business owner's success. They just don't how to succeed. I didn't say *they don't know how to do their job*... That is the easy part for them. The problem is they don't actually know how to win. Their personal filter is holding them back. It is making bad decisions every day. It is making bad decisions about the people they are listening to. It is making bad decisions about getting the help they need. They have a failure filter.

I have a friend who runs a real estate agency. He is the most talented person I know in that industry. He has vision, style, and amazing interior design skills. He can take a beaten down broken shell of a house in a crappy neighborhood, "Imagineer it" (to quote Disney) and rebuild it into something that people will fight to buy. It's truly amazing.

Here is the problem; he is maybe the worst businessperson I know. He absolutely cannot handle the details of the business side of the operation. His books are a mess. The bills aren't paid. Taxes haven't been filed in years. He is always struggling for money and has no idea how to fix any of it. He is NOT a manager or an entrepreneur. He is a specialist. He is really good at being a specialist, but he needs to bring in a manager or CEO.

The bigger problem is that he won't listen. He is stubborn and has a failure filter. He has absolutely no idea how to fix the problems he knows he has.

That's because he has never really experienced success and has failed so many times that he doesn't understand how to win.

He is like a person trying to walk from one room to the next by going through the wall instead of the door. You could point out the door to him, and his personal failure filter would reject the answer about where the door is. He would then argue with you about why that door wouldn't work and why going through the wall is the only option. He would watch you walk back and forth through the door over and over again and still say he needs to go through the wall. His failure filter absolutely rejects that what he is watching you do...will work for him. He wants to do it his way. It's maddening to watch.

If my friend would just listen to good advice and bring in the right person to manage the business side of the company or hire a consultant to straighten his business out, he would probably make ten times the amount of money he makes now and grow a huge and very successful organization. My friend is destined to fail again and again because he refuses to learn and won't accept input from anyone else who has a success filter and can show him the right way. His failure filter is strong.

Business Lesson #8... *PLEASE understand that if you aren't succeeding in what you're doing, you probably have a strong failure filter that is making the wrong decisions for you about what you should be doing. You are fighting an uphill battle that you probably will not win.*

If someone is showing you where the door is, DONT keep trying to walk through the wall. It will not work.

CHAPTER 5

THE PROBLEM WITH SALESPEOPLE AND MANAGERS

"The harder the conflict, the more glorious the triumph."
–Thomas Paine

Salespeople - How Hard Can It be to Push Paper?

Specialists are not the only ones having issues when starting a new business. Salespeople have issues, too, and often they are the same ones that specialists deal with.

Salespeople go out every day and generate new sales. Those sales bring in revenue. Salespeople can usually also see the profit margins on their sales, and they get paid a small commission on those profits. This sets up the perfect scenario for the salesperson to hit the roof and yell: *"The company is making so much money off me; If I owned the company, I could make ALL the money. They wouldn't even have a company if I didn't go out there and make all the sales. I am the most important person here!"* I have heard this in my companies a hundred times. It always makes me laugh.

Back in 1997-99, I started my first online insurance agency and hired a guy named Craig to work for me as a salesperson. He was one of our best salespeople and made a pretty good living. He was also very high maintenance. Craig always complained that his sales leads were not good enough or that the insurance company was not giving his clients a fair shake in underwriting. He would complain that the office staff wasn't doing enough to support him, and they needed to understand he was the top dog. I understood this type of high maintenance behavior came with the territory when working with high performers, so our staff did our best to keep him happy.

When I sold the company in 1999, Craig came into the office and asked me how much of the sales price he was going to get. I asked him what he meant by that. He told me that since he was responsible for a portion of the sales we did, that he was entitled to that portion of the sales price. I told him that he was not an owner of the company and would not get any of the money.

Craig was incredulous. He just could not believe that he was not entitled to the money. I told him that he had not set the company up. He had not risked his money or racked up debt to finance operations when there was not enough money to pay the bills. He had not paid employees out of his pocket with no guarantee of getting it back when the company was starting. He hadn't worked seven days a week to manage the business and had no idea what it had taken to get our business to the point where it could even be sold. He got paid every week, even when we didn't make any money.

In short, I related that he was an employee, not an owner, then suggested that he could come work for the new owner if he wanted to so he could continue to make a great living.

Well, Craig got mad and quit. He told me he was going to build his own company. Within a few weeks, he started an agency and was in business.

I ran into Craig a few years later. He had not lasted long on his own and was out of business and working in another industry. He told me that the insurance business had changed. He couldn't catch a break and blah, blah, blah, blah, blah. Of course, it was everyone else's fault but his own.

Craig didn't have a clue what it took to actually build or run a business. He thought you simply sold something, and everything else was easy. He could have stayed on with us when we sold and kept his income and lifestyle. He could have come back after his business failed and gotten his old job back, but he was too proud to do that, and his ego got in the way.

Similar to our specialist in the above chapter, salespeople start businesses based on their sales talents, only to have the same backend challenges. They know how to make sales, and in their minds, believe sales is the most important aspect of the business. For the most part, they are right.

However…

This would be similar to believing the engine in a car is the most important part of the car. It is true that the engine is what makes the car run and that the type of engine can make a car go fast or slow. And we all know that without an engine, the car will not move.

Consider this; the engine is even more important if you own a racecar. You need a high-performance engine to win races. The challenge here is that no matter how awesome the engine is, even if it cost $200,000, without four simple tires, your car goes nowhere. Your car is just going to sit there revving its engine. Now imagine taking out the steering wheel in your race car. Your car will crash within the first few seconds of driving it. Imagine you're a race car taking off at one hundred miles an hour when you're heading into a turn, and you have no brakes. You're a dead man. The engine may be important, but without the rest of the parts, your car is just a huge paperweight stuck in the driveway going nowhere. It's useless. Don't even think about trying to drive it. It will end badly.

This same principle applies to your business. You need sales, and great salespeople are invaluable, but If you don't have the right team behind them making sure the organization actually runs, your business will eventually fail. The parts on this racecar are similar to the roles in your company.

Salespeople, unfortunately, tend to forget the support staff that makes them successful, and they don't appreciate them.

They tend to think hiring and managing specialists is easy. In their mind, *anybody can be a specialist and do the physical labor.* They also may believe managers are glorified paper pushers who complicate their lives by slowing the process down with a bunch of details. In their opinion, their job is paperwork only, and anybody can do that; it's just an office job.

It is the over-inflated ego of the gun-slinging salesperson that gets them into trouble in business. They don't do details, and details are what makes everything actually work.

A smart salesperson takes care of their office staff. They buy them coffee in the morning and spring for lunch every now and then. A smart salesperson understands that the support staff (the wheels, the steering wheel, and the brakes on the racecar) are critical. Without them, the engine is useless.

Business Lesson #9... *Salespeople generally don't understand what it takes to make the entire company work. There will be Craigs who work for you. They will feel entitled to what you have. They may even quit and try to go out on their own. Let them. Once that attitude of entitlement gets too strong, they will become a cancer to the organization. Let them go, but keep the door open for when they fail. Chances are they will not make it, and you may get a new and improved employee back — one whose ego is in check.*

Managers

Managers start businesses because they think they make everything happen. They manage all the details. They see everything behind the scenes. Managers run the actual company and feel like everything else is the easy part. Where managers really get into trouble is when they go out and try to sell. Managers tend to think that salespeople are overrated and that selling is easy. They think it is a black and white process that relies on fact presentation. That is not what sales is about, and that type of presentation just doesn't work.

Shortly after Mitch and I sold the first project for the new software division we had launched, our company CEO suddenly got excited about what we were doing. This was the same guy who, after purchasing my company, told me I wasn't qualified to run it and hired a "young, sharp MBA" to take over my job. He then demoted me to a sales manager position. After seeing our initial success in sales selling a new concept and product, he decided once again that I wasn't qualified to sell software or the new product and made the decision to hand the project over to our VP of Business Development, Kyle, and the VP of Sales, LJ. They took an immediate interest in the new project. Since our project appeared to be the newest and greatest thing, they wanted to get a piece of it.

Our third and fourth presentation for this new platform was already set up out in California. LJ and Kyle came to me and told me that they would be taking over the new division and sales presentation, and I was no longer needed. You have to remember that this was a young startup dot-com and that all the employees had MBAs ... except me. I was just the guy whose company they'd bought, and I had **no education**. Obviously, they could do a better job selling software than me, right? (Even though I had come up with the new concept and gotten it to the point where people could actually use it and we could make money.)

> **So, off they went to California without me. I was not happy. This entire project was mine. I had written the business plan. I had developed the model. I had built the sales presentation and sold the first project. It was going to be my future.**

The trip consisted of a two-day presentation. Kyle, LJ, and Mitch were giving the presentation to two large insurance carriers. I remember being angry as I sat in the office the next day, thinking about not being there. I was talking to our CFO when I got a 911 call on my pager and then on my cell phone. It was Mitch calling from California. I picked up the phone and asked how they were doing. Mitch said, "You have to get on the first flight to Cali! We are bombing, and I need you here." I asked what was going on. He said Kyle and LJ didn't have a clue how to sell the platform, and they were about to lose the deal.

I hung up and told the CFO about the call. He told me to go home, grab some clothes and get to the airport. So, I jumped on a plane and headed to Mountain View.

I met with Mitch that night to find out what was happening. He told me that Kyle and LJ had no idea how to sell or handle a room. They were managers, not salespeople. They thought the process of sales was about explaining facts.

They just didn't get it.

Once Mitch knew the ship was sinking, he made an excuse halfway through the presentation about some technical problem and asked if they could reconvene the next day. That's when he called me. I was going to go in and start from scratch and do our normal drill we had learned from the first several presentations.

The next day I walked into the combat zone. About twenty people sat at a long table facing me. They all had their arms folded and were waiting to see what the new guy was going to say. It was a hostile environment!!

I made a decision on the spot not to pitch them and that talking was not going to work; they had already wasted a day on the presentation the day before, and half of them had probably already made up their mind.

So, we pivoted, and instead of talking "at them," I walked over and sat down at the table with them, ignoring both the Power-Point presentation on the screen, as well as the rest of our team. I asked them questions. Instead of trying to sell them something, I started connecting with them on a more personal level. I remember sitting there in that chair talking and seeing our team over on the side of the room, looking at each other in confusion. Their expressions clearly read: *what the hell is he doing?*

That simple act of connecting with the group got them talking. I found out their pain points. Over the next hour or so, they told me exactly what they needed ... and then I showed them how I could fix their problems with our brand new "never been done before" magic software platform.

We left that day with a happy group of people and ended up closing that deal a week or so later for over $2 million in revenue.

Don't get me wrong; I had nothing to do with the actual closing documents and contracts, etc. My job was done. Kyle and LJ wrapped up the paperwork. They did what they were good at... managing.

The problem was that Kyle and LJ were managers. They *thought* they were salespeople, but they weren't. LJ's title was even the VP of sales, but I don't think she could sell anything to anyone. **Sales is a very specific skillset with multiple levels of ability**. For the most part, you either have it, or you don't.

I want to reiterate that managers are critically important to the organization. As a salesperson, I have absolutely no desire to manage the details, and I hate paperwork. I need managers ... but I also need managers to understand their role — so we all win.

Likewise, when managers start companies, they also need to understand their role and bring in the right people to handle the rest.

Business Lesson #10... *If someone else can do it better than you, drop your ego and let them. Your chance of success is better. And here is the best part ... you win either way!!*

CHAPTER 6

INCOME COLUMN
VS. EXPENSE COLUMN

"Beware of little expenses. A small leak will sink a great ship." –Benjamin Franklin

Sales is one of my favorite topics. As I stated earlier, sales makes the world go around. Without sales, you don't have a company. Without sales, you don't have anything. Sales really does make the entire world's economic engine run.

Before we jump into the meat and bones of the chapter, let's start with a hard-learned rule.

Great salespeople do not make great sales managers. And great sales managers are probably not great salespeople. These are two different personalities and two different skillsets.

It is because of this distinction that promoting your salespeople to a sales manager position is usually what we call being promoted down. When this happens, the salesperson has more "details" responsibility and will probably make less money. I have rarely seen this work effectively. Sales management jobs should go to a manager, not a gun-slinging rainmaker.

I have always taught my managers the theory of the "expense and income columns." Every company, at its core, is just a Profit and Loss statement (P&L).

A P&L is made up of two areas: revenue by category and expenses by category. Everyone and everything in the company fits into one of these two categories. This includes every single person in the company. I see business owners assume all the time that since payroll is an expense, all people are an expense. This is only half true.

Some people cost the company money, and some people make the company money.

It is true that the actual dollars of a salesperson's payroll are an expense at a macro level, but the actual salespeople themselves are revenue generators.

Conceptually, each Salesperson has an **"individual P&L."**

This individual P&L actually operates as a mini P&L at the micro level, inside the company's overall P&L, which is at a macro level. That mini P&L has income and expenses and should generate a profit for the company. I call this strategy "BOTTOM UP management and P&L analysis."

In other words, if we look at the physical numbers on the spreadsheet, the individual's salary is an expense, but when we break that P&L down to a micro level, it gives you an entirely new way of looking at your company.

Again, everybody in the company is in one column or the other.

Salespeople generate revenue because you have a product or a service, and they sell that product or service to your end consumer. Those sales generate revenue that covers their salary as well as provides enough to contribute to the company's overall expenses. That's why salespeople go into the income column of your company.

Specialists are also in the income column. They go out and perform the work, and that generates revenue.

Managers, VPs, admin personnel, the CEO, and everyone else in the company cost money and bring nothing in to offset it. They are in the expense column. They are support personnel.

At an overly simplified level, we could fire all these support people, and we would still have revenue from the salespeople and the specialists. We would still be in business (for a little while). However, if we fired all the salespeople and specialists, we would be out of business. We would have no revenue, and nobody would get paid.

So ... who is more important in pretty much any company?

And ... what category do you fit into inside your company?

When my third company was acquired by a venture capital company out of Silicon Valley, I spent about a year going back and forth between Atlanta, Georgia, and San Jose, California, the home of Sand Hill Road—the heart and soul of Silicon Valley.

We were absorbed into one of the portfolio companies of this VC firm. It was an eye-opening experience for a kid who had barely graduated high school. The first time I walked into the board room of our largest investor, I saw a bunch of plaques on the wall. Each plaque represented a deal they had done and exited. There were statements like "XYZ company purchased for $50 million went public and cashed out at $500 million." This VC firm was an early investor in Facebook, LinkedIn, and a whole bunch of other companies I had never heard of. They had made billions for their investors, and I was in awe!

The atmosphere in Silicon Valley is all about the engineers. The ones I met were super smart and the highest-paid people in the valley. They developed new and exciting software that would, or could, change the world. I also found these engineers to be super ego-inflated. They believed that engineering positions were the only important positions that needed to be filled in the companies where they worked. They had the mindset that they were the only ones who mattered.

I routinely had discussions with some of these engineers I worked with about the fact that it didn't matter how good their new twist on programming was; somebody still had to sell the end product.

If nobody sold it, the company would cease to exist. I can't tell you how many of those guys never got that point. They just assumed if they built something, someone would come along and buy it. With that warped mindset, it's not surprising how many failed.

Business Lesson #11... *It really doesn't matter what your title is or how smart you are. Without sales, you have nothing.*

I have also had many discussions about sales and salespeople with managers in both my company and in the different companies where I have consulted. Remember what I said about salespeople. They are ego-driven. They eat what they kill. They thrive on the chase and push boundaries to the very limit. Then they hang one foot over the line in the sand, pretending like nobody sees them doing it. They are thoroughbreds. But they are also flakey, unpredictable, moody, and will try to get away with things they know they shouldn't.

These things drive managers crazy. Managers always want to come down on the salespeople who won't toe the line exactly the way they tell them to. The inability and refusal to adhere to rules is infuriating to a process-and-procedure-driven person. They just don't get it. A typical conversation might go like this:

Manager – Brian, we have to do something about Jeff!!

Me – Why, what happened?

Manager – Jeff told a client something he shouldn't have and then didn't do his paperwork right! Now my team has to clean up his mess, and I'm tired of cleaning up after Jeff!!

Me – Well, how bad is it…? Is what he did illegal?

Manager – NO! But that isn't the point. We have procedures around here that Jeff knows he needs to follow, and he isn't doing it! I'm tired of arguing with him about this.

Me – Isn't Jeff our top salesperson?

Manager – Yes, and again, that's not the point! You can't just let these salespeople do whatever they want! We have rules!

Me – Let me ask you something… If Jeff didn't sell anything, what would your team have to do?

Manager – What do you mean?

Me – Not a hard question. If Jeff didn't sell anything, what would your team have to do?

Manager – Ummm...nothing...

Me – If Jeff did everything exactly right...what would your team have to do again?

Manager – A lot less work!!!

Me – OK... So, what you're saying is if I didn't need you to clean up after Jeff ... then I wouldn't need you at all??!!

Manager – What??!!

Me – Listen to me. Jeff is who he is, and he generates a lot of revenue. Jeff's sales pay your salary. Your job is to make sure Jeff keeps generating revenue. Jeff is in the income column here, and quite frankly, you should be glad Jeff needs you to clean up his mess because if Jeff doesn't need you, then I don't need you. You, my friend, are in the expense column!

Manager – I will be in my office...

Business Lesson #12... *People in the revenue (income) column get a certain amount of leeway. (Although we generally don't tell them that.) So, be careful you don't run off your rainmakers with too many silly rules that frustrate them, so they eventually have to take their skill and your revenue to another company.*

CHAPTER 7
IF YOU CAN'T STAND THE HEAT...

"Failure is often that early morning hour of darkness which precedes the dawning of the day of success." –Leigh Mitchell Hodges

Starting and operating a business is hard. I know it sounds glamourous to a lot of people who are sitting in an office dreaming of owning their own company. Endless infomercials on TV tell you that you need to break free and do your own thing and get rich.

On the outside, it appears that all these businesses are making a lot of money, but the reality is that most are not. Fifty percent fail in the first couple of years, and people lose a lot of money. Owners tend to be stressed out most of the time because there are always problems.

They come in the form of things like your employees, customers, the government, or your personal finances. Problems pop up daily.

The other issue is that business owners can't really go home at five o clock and forget about work until the next day. Yesterday's problems are still there at the end of the typical working day and tomorrow promises even more problems to come. It never ends.

Don't get me wrong...

I love being in business.

I love the freedom that it gives me, but I also understand the challenges, and at this point, I'm not that surprised when things go sideways or even backward.

It's all part of the game.

My first business was a landscaping company. I started it in Ohio right after I got married, but several months after launching it, I moved to Atlanta to be closer to my National Guard unit based out of Dobbins Air Force Base. I was around twenty-two years old, and I hustled my tail off.

The first big account I signed was for a commercial office park of around a dozen buildings. We cut the grass and maintained the landscaping. Each of the buildings was privately owned, although we technically worked for the management company that oversaw the property. The property manager was William, and he was a nice guy. William took a chance on a very young kid to take care of his property. I was very grateful for that.

The problem was with a dozen building owners; someone was always unhappy with the work we did. They constantly complained to William about it.

William would then call me into the office to go over the complaints. It was never-ending.

One day William called me about a complaint from one of the owners. I was having a particularly bad day. After the normal pleasantries, he started to explain the problems we needed to address. Suddenly he stopped talking about all the issues and asked me if something was wrong. He must've seen the frown on my face. I told William that the owners were being ridiculous. They all wanted something different and never stopped com- plaining.

I will never forget the next thing William told me. It has stuck with me my entire business career.

The conversation I had with William that day, I have had with many people who have worked for me over the last thirty- five years.

William said, "Brian, let me tell you something. This is the career you chose. These are the issues that go along with that career. This is just the way it is, and it's never going to change. So, you have a choice. You can either deal with it and move on with your business or **if you can't stand the heat, get out of the kitchen** and quit. But complaining about it is a waste of your time and mine."

That was one of the moments in life where you hear some- thing, and it hits you. You know in that instant, you are either going to **man up or fold up**, that it's time to make a choice.

That is William's legacy to me, and it has served me well. On a side note, I now own a building in that office park, and William is still there ... and still a very nice man!

Every time I have dealt with a similar circumstance like this, where it's not just hot in the kitchen, but the kitchen actually appears to be burning down, I remember that time with William in his office.

The point is that you are going to run across situations like this often in your own business. Things will go wrong. People will steal from you. People will quit. Contracts won't pay you. Someone will sue you for something you didn't do and outright lie to a judge … and you will lose. Things will get crazy.

I have had so many kitchen fires in my business career that I should be a volunteer fireman! More accurately, I should be an involuntary fireman!

You will encounter the same kinds of problems that will require you to figure out the solutions. It's best to get used to the inevitable.

My landscaping company did both maintenance and installation. Early on in my landscaping days, one of our jobs started as a contract to landscape a man's backyard. In the middle of the job, we signed another separate contract to landscape his front yard.

When we completed the backyard and tried to collect our fee, he refused to pay us the entire amount. He said that he had decided the price was too high. We argued about it briefly. He was going to short me around $500 on the job. I was angry but decided it wasn't worth arguing about, and the amount was too little to sue for so, I walked away. I also told him I was not going to do his front yard project since he hadn't paid in full on the backyard. I left and didn't think about it again for another month.

Then one day, I was hanging out with my family at my house when the sheriff showed up. Now where I live, when the sheriff shows up, it's because you are being served with a lawsuit. Sure enough, I was being sued by the guy who hadn't paid me. But he was suing me for "specific performance" for not fulfilling the contract on the front yard. I had given him a price of $4500. He then went and had another company do the job and paid them $6500. So, he had decided to sue me for the $2000 difference.

Being young and naïve, I figured this was an easy case. I would simply explain to the judge what had happened, and it would get thrown out.

I had no idea what was about to go down. The judge found in his favor and awarded him the $2000 plus court costs, etc. I pleaded with the judge and told him the guy hadn't paid the last contract price. The judge told me that I should sue him for it, but that case had nothing to do with this one. I lost. I also learned a very valuable lesson about how contracts work. I never made that mistake again. I didn't win that day. I learned.

I cannot tell you how angry I was walking out of court. The world was not fair. The judge was not fair. The guy who sued me and won was a horrible person. Nothing about this was ever going to be alright. So, there I was; it was decision time. I had to give the guy who screwed me out of $500 ... another $2000 that I didn't have.

How are you going to handle yourself when everything and everybody comes down on you? And trust me, it will, and they will ... and it will probably happen more than once. When your world is crumbling around you, are you going to man up or fold up? Are you going to let it ruin everything else in your life?? The choice is yours.

Business Lesson #13... *Mentally prepare yourself for the kitchen fires. They will happen, and you probably won't see them coming.*

CHAPTER 8

WHY ARE YOU HERE?

"Nobody forces you to work at Wal-Mart. Start
your own business! Sell something to Wal-Mart!"
–Kevin O'Leary

OK, so far, we have talked about some of the obstacles you either will or are encountering in your business.

We have discussed the personalities of the people you need to hire to grow your business from a startup to a thriving business you can scale.

Hopefully, you have realized that you can't just stick anyone into the roles you need filling if that is not who they are. Hopefully, you have also decided that you're here to stay, even if the entire kitchen and the rest of the house are going up in flames!

Now let's talk about why you're here.

Why did you decide to start your own business?

Why are you willing to go through the pain and BS it will take to succeed?

Why do you want this headache when it would be so much easier to get a job and collect a check?

A job can give you:

a. A Steady income
b. Stability
c. Benefits

d. No worries about making payroll

e. A 401(k)

f. Vacation time

g. No worries that you will get sued

h. No customers calling you at home at night

i. No needy employees asking you for advances on pay (that you never get back)

j. No stress about the fact that one week you can't pay yourself because you have to take care of your employees first

Having a job is so much easier.

So why are you doing this?

I can list a bunch of reasons to be in business...

a. The hope of making a ton of money (but remember, 30% of new businesses fail in the first year)

b. The freedom you think you will have as your own boss (*but ... now every customer is your boss*)

c. The idea that you can do it better than anyone else (*perhaps, but there is always someone better*)

d. Maybe you need to prove something to yourself (*be careful that what you end up proving isn't what you thought it was going to be*)

e. You have a passion (*most things you do for fun stop being fun when you have to make a living doing them*)

f. You saw your friend start a business and make a boatload of money (*be sure your friend isn't Facebook successful. Everyone on Facebook looks happy and successful. And we know that just isn't true!! Or maybe your friend is successful and has that magical quality that successful people have ... but do you have it?)*

There are a whole host of other reasons to go into business for yourself.

I want to know...what is yours? What is going to make you do what's necessary to stay in the fight? What drives you forward?

Being in business is sometimes grueling, so... Maybe you should get a job instead. Or maybe you should keep your job. It might be the safer play and better for your family.

It's going to be hard.

Your chances of success are not that good, and it's probably not worth the risk.

You could lose your savings.

You'll cause all kinds of stress on your family.

You could put your marriage at risk.

SO... *Why* in the world would you want to take all those chances??!!

Seriously... Don't do it... You will probably fail... It's not worth it!!!

Does all that make sense???

OR

Does that statement make you mad?

Does a feeling well up inside you that says this guy has no idea what he's talking about!?!

That was a test...

How did you do?

Did you find out that you really want it?

If you don't have absolute confidence in yourself, you shouldn't start your own business.

If you do, and if everything inside you tells you this is the right thing and that you don't just want to do this, but you absolutely need to do this, then let's get started...

Business Lesson #14... *You better really want this, or you shouldn't do it. Seriously, unless you can't live without it, don't do it.*

.

CHAPTER 9

CLUELESS TENACITY

"Learning is the eye of the mind." -French Proverb

Definition of Clueless Tenacity: *It is the ability to take an opportunity or idea and run with it when you have absolutely no idea what you're doing.*

This may very well be the theme of my life. In every career path I have started down, I've had absolutely no idea what I was doing.

After I started a landscaping company and sold my first job, I had to ask a friend to come and teach me how to plant bushes correctly. I had never done it before.

I am willing to bet that there are over one hundred homes in the North Fulton County, Georgia area that have the exact same landscape design with the exact same bushes planted in their front yard in the exact same places. I knew very little about plants, so I sold the same plants and the same design over and over and over. As long as those clients weren't neighbors, it all worked out!

When I started selling insurance, I went on one sales call with my friend and then started the next day. I was a clueless landscaper by day and clueless insurance expert with one day's worth of experience by night.

When I started selling software, I didn't even know how it worked. I took along a guy who was way smarter than me to answer the technical questions.

When I bought my first restaurant, I didn't and still don't know how to cook. I don't know how to make drinks. I don't know how to use the POS (Point of Sale) ordering system. I don't know anything about seating charts or how a kitchen operates. I literally don't know how to run a restaurant at all. But I have seven of them now doing around $9 million in revenue … and two more under construction.

But none of my inexperience mattered.

I never allowed my lack of knowledge or understanding to stop me from taking an opportunity and running with it.

Back in my early days of landscaping, I was mowing the grass around a bunch of warehouses at an Army supply base in Atlanta. These warehouses were a shipping out point for a lot of other bases in the US and around the world.

One day, the man in charge of the warehouses came to me and said, "Brian, you seem like an industrious kind of guy. I have an opportunity that I want to see if you can help me with." I said, "Sure, what are we talking about?"

He took me inside one of the warehouses and showed me four thousand cases of sports drink. He told me they had been shipped from this base over to Kuwait for Desert Storm. By the time they got there, however, the war was over, and the troops were coming home, so they shipped all four thousand cases back to his warehouse.

He asked me if I would be interested in taking them off his hands. He did not care what I did with them, he just needed them gone, and the manufacturer didn't want them back. He even suggested that I sell them to a pig farmer to mix in with their slop. If I could get rid of them for him, he would give me all four thousand cases for five cents each … $200. The man even told me he would ship them anywhere I wanted them to go for free.

Each case had twelve bottles. So, we are talking about 48,000 bottles. I did the calculations. If I bought that many at the store, it would have cost me $100,000. I had enough sports drink to fill a small swimming pool.

Before I made the commitment and bought the whole lot, I asked him for about a dozen cases to see what I could do with them. He threw them in my truck, and I left. On my way home, I stopped by a gas station because I wondered if they would be interested in buying some cases of sports drink. I asked the guy at the counter, and he asked me how much I was selling them for. I told him $2.50 a case, and I had as many as he wanted.

He asked me where I got them, and I told him; then he said he would get back to me.

I didn't know it at the time, but that gas station was owned by a guy who had about a dozen gas stations.

The owner called me back and asked if the drinks were safe to drink. I told him I would find out.

So, I got out a Yellow Pages and looked up an FDA laboratory in Atlanta. Then I called them and asked how much it would cost me to have my sample cases tested. They quoted me about $200. I took them in that day.

I got a call back from the lab a couple of days later. They had tested the bottles against random bottles from multiple locations around the Atlanta area, and there was absolutely no difference between what I had and what was on the shelves around town. The lab certified that they were safe, and I was on to the second part of my plan.

I called the owner back and told him I had the letter from the FDA certifying the drinks. He bought all four thousand cases from me and gave me a check for $10,000. They were shipped to his warehouse. I couldn't believe I'd just made $10,000 in a couple of days by doing almost nothing.

I'd had absolutely no idea what I was going to do when I was given that opportunity, but I took it and then went out and figured it out.

Richard Branson has a book called *Screw It, Let's Do It*. I loved that book. It basically says the same thing I'm telling you: if you're given an opportunity, take it and figure out how to do it later.

Business Lesson #15... *Don't let the mere prospect of having* **NO CLUE** *about what you're doing stop you from pursuing your dreams and ideas. Sometimes you just have to go for it. And then be tenacious about it while you figure it out.*

CHAPTER 10

BUSINESS IS BOTH
AN ART AND A SCIENCE

*"Being good in business is the most fascinating
kind of art. Making money is art, and working is
art, and good business is the best art."*
—Andy Warhol

In this chapter, we will start getting into the nuts and bolts of building a company that you can scale.

We will break down what you need to really get your business going. Let's start with the "art" side of your company, aka the touchy-feely or cerebral part.

To figure out what this looks like for you, answer these questions:

What do you do?

What product do you sell, or what service do you provide?

Why is your product, service, or customer service better?

Why should I buy this from you instead of someone else?

That last question is maybe the most critical question you should ask yourself. If the answer doesn't roll off your tongue, you need to spend some time trying to figure it out.

These are critical questions you need to answer before you can effectively market yourself to the public.

If you don't know the absolute answer, then the public won't either, and you will be just another business trying to hustle a buck.

Let me give you three examples of what I'm talking about here.

Recently I got a call from a guy who used to work for me selling insurance. He had started his own agency and was getting ready for the open enrollment season. He asked me for some advice on getting in the door to pitch his product and services to different companies. He was looking for an open line or his pitch.

I said that's easy, but first, tell me as a customer, "Why should I buy from you?"

He said, "Because I offer great customer service."

My response was, "So what? That's what everyone says. Why are you better than them?" (People hate it when I ask this!)

He responded, "Because I care about you and your employees."

Again, I said, "That's what everyone says. Why do you care more than anyone else?"

At this point, he didn't have an answer. I told him to figure out the answer to that question first … and then we would talk. (Truthfully, if he figured out that answer as to why people should buy from him, he didn't need to talk to me anymore.)

Here's why…

When you figure out the "why" question, you will have your opening pitch. He was looking for a magic bullet pitch line that didn't exist.

What he needed instead was to figure out why anyone would want to buy from him. He needed to know what was he offering that somebody else didn't have? This is the hard part about getting started. If your business is just another dime a dozen, you will never scale.

My second example of "why" is an easy one.

I recently built and opened a new restaurant in the town where I live. The new downtown development that was being built is what we like to call a "live, work, and play" community. Technically it's called a mixed-use development, but I like my way of saying it better.

I live there and can walk out my front door and hit a dozen restaurants, a gym, all kinds of shops, a barbershop, a spa, and large green spaces to hang out in with my friends. We never have to leave.

When we looked at this area to assess where we wanted to put the restaurant, it already had ten restaurants within about one hundred yards of the space we wanted. They had high-end seafood. They had a wine bar. They had Indian food and a brewery. There were lots of options. This community was also surrounded by about 50,000 homes within a 3-square-mile radius with walking paths leading to the downtown area.

We noticed that not one of the restaurants had TVs. Nobody was playing sports in the restaurants, and it was football season. We also noticed that nobody sold domestic beer. They all served craft beer. We talked to people in the area, and everyone kept telling us the same thing, "We need a sports tavern. We want a place to hang out and watch a game and have fun."

With that in mind, we built a 4000-sq-ft sports bar with an indoor-outdoor seating area and installed twenty-six large flat-screen TVs both inside and out on the patio. We got the most comfortable chairs we could find and surrounded the extra-large bar with thirty-two of them. And we had domestic beer!

Our restaurant was different than everyone else's. We didn't have any competition within five miles.

That's why we are different and why people come to us. We are not just another restaurant. We are the only place close by where you can sit and watch the game and drink a domestic beer.

My last example of "why" is about my editor.

When I was shopping for an editor for my last book, I looked at a few different larger companies that I had been referred to. One, in particular, I really liked, and I had made up my mind to use them. I then got one last referral from a friend.

I contacted this referral, Hilary, and shared with her what I was doing and the companies I was looking at. I told her that I really liked the one company in particular. She was very knowl-edgeable about the industry and the job and knew the company I mentioned well. She told me that she had talked to them about working for them in the past as a subcontractor but ultimately had decided against it and chose to keep growing her own company. She told me her fee structure and that she felt like this company overcharged their clients and that she could be more cost-effective. I would get exactly the same thing this company was selling me for less money.

This hit home.

I realized this company was basically going to take my money and then subcontract out the work to someone like Hilary. I would be paying a middleman. I would not get any more value. With Hilary's deal, I would be using the same person (or a similar person) that I would have used at that company, but now, I would be working with the subcontractor directly and saving money.

Bingo ... this is what she was offering me that I couldn't get anyplace else. I was getting the same exact service at a lower cost. I chose Hilary and have been super glad I did.

She had answered my question, "Why should I buy from you instead of someone else?"

It wasn't just the cheaper price she gave me. She actually gave me the EXACT same thing the bigger company would have given me ... at a lower price.

I actually wonder if she knew that this was the answer to the question, "Why should someone come to your business?" Did she know she was giving me the actual "why," or did she think she was just pitching me a price? I don't know... I haven't asked her yet...

We've now wound up back at the first step, and you still need to answer the question I posed above. Be honest with yourself.

If you are selling the same exact service as someone else, then you need to differentiate yourself in some way.

Answer the question to the best of your ability and test your answers on your friends. It may take a while to get the right answer, but when you do, you will have something you can launch and start to scale.

Business Lesson #16... *Answer the "why."*

CHAPTER 11

RUNNING THE NUMBERS —THE SCIENCE

"Math is fun. It teaches you life and death information. Like when you're cold, you should go to a corner since it's ninety degrees there."
–Old Joke

The thing that most amazes me when I talk to or consult with a business owner is that a lot of them do not have clean P&Ls that they use to manage their business.

I have acquired a dozen restaurants in the last ten years, and when we begin negotiations, I always ask for the last 12-24 months of P&L statements broken down by month on a single spreadsheet with all categories visible.

Nine times out of ten, a business doesn't have it. The business owner I'm talking to has likely never looked at their P&Ls as real time management tools. They've only regarded them as a grade card. This is a huge mistake.

Generally speaking, when asked about their P&L, most owners have to go to their bookkeeper and see if they can create that report. That is AMAZING to me!!

How do you run a company if you have no idea what the numbers are??

You should be studying your numbers. They will tell you virtually everything you need to know about your business. They will tell you how you did in the past and how you're going to do in the future. They are like magic crystal ball numbers.

As it relates to our restaurants ... every morning, when I get up, I check all the bank accounts to make sure nothing weird happened the prior night and get a sense of our cash position.

I can also access daily sales and labor reports at any time, in real-time, via an online app. This app shows me sales and labor reports as they occur, as well as percentage comparisons to the past week or month. The key here is to pay attention to what is trending.

Trends in time can spotlight subtle issues that you can't see on the surface and what isn't super visual every day. This app is also programmed to send me a text alert if any of my employees give away free food or alcohol over a certain amount. It also tells me if their tips are extraordinarily high on a particular check. The app watches and records everything for me.

I also get copied on all weekly food and liquor orders the managers are purchasing, as well as copies of all the schedules, including the projected labor for the week. I know what the general range of expenditures should be by location and the set labor budget number we are supposed to stay under. This is my counter-check to make sure they are on track.

My accounting department sends me interim monthly P&Ls every Thursday for all my companies, along with all outstanding bills recorded in a set of Excel reports. While these numbers are not absolute, they are close and allow me to see what is going on in real-time. At the end of the month, we get a full set of P&Ls and balance sheets as well as a cash position and the cash accumulation or cash burn.

If you think this sounds like a lot of data, it is. However, it takes me probably an hour a day to check it all.

The best part is I can do all of it on my phone from anywhere in the world.

I don't have to be in an office or at any of the locations to know exactly what is going on in them.

If any of the numbers don't fit into the range I expect, I make a call and have someone start looking into it. If all the numbers are on track, I know we will make a certain profit percentage on our revenue. This can be predictably tracked. Add to this the fact that I have a camera system in all locations that I can access on my phone, and I can literally be anywhere and everywhere all the time.

Data and P&Ls are your friends and a critical part of your business. Without them, you are flying blind while hoping you make money. They are the roadmap to past trends and future profits. I could never step foot in any of my locations again and still run the companies well, all because I have good data.

Business Lesson #17... *If you don't have the right kind of data on your business, that is the first thing you need to figure out how to get.*

CHAPTER 12

P&L BY PERSON—OH NO, HERE COMES THE MATH!! AND MORE SCIENCE

"It's not what you pay a person, but what they cost you that counts." —Will Rogers

In this chapter, we are going to do some analysis on the income side of your P&L. Remember, everyone who works for you is either in the income or expense column.

Have you ever analyzed your workforce in this way?

Have you ever thought about the fact that each salesperson has their own individual P&L ... and that individual P&Ls flow up to the overall P&L and make up your success or failure?

I call running your business in this way "Managing your company from the bottom up."

Are you ready to do some math?

I can already envision some of you rolling your eyes and thinking... *MATH ... I hate MATH...* While I understand that sentiment, you need to understand that the math is critical to your business.

If you're a math person, you're gonna love this section... If you're not, your eyes are going to glaze over.

However, if you're not a math person, you REALLY need to find someone who is and have them do the math and give it to you in easy-to-read snippets so you are aware of what's going on. This will allow you to make quality decisions about what you need to do to either fix your issues or get better at what you do.

My favorite thing about math is that it doesn't lie. The numbers are what they are. They will tell you everything.

I am going to start getting a bit more technical in just a moment but stay with me here. What I am going to cover next is usually better taught on a whiteboard, but since we can't do that here, I am going to try to make this as simple as I can.

What we go over in this chapter applies to any organization of any size with salespeople (people in the income column).

I have done this with small companies and HUGE companies; the largest was a $2 billion insurance carrier.

In the following example, I was hired by a company on the West Coast to come in and overhaul their operations. They had about eighty salespeople working for them at the time, as well as an entire floor of support staff. They were doing probably $50-60 million annually in sales. On the surface, they looked quite successful. But this company was like most companies I find; they had the data needed in various reports, but nobody was watching it or learning from it. They were not profitable.

Before I get into the details, we first need to establish some background information for this exercise.

The sales activity in your organization is broken down here into several parts for clarity. For this part, we will discuss the math behind:

- Sales leads
- Sales calls
- Close rate

Sales Leads

I am discussing a telephone sales center here, but these numbers could just as easily be converted to an outside sales organization. If you aren't sure how to execute this, you need to find someone who can consult for you and set this type of tracking up.

When I got the contract with this large company, they were buying sale leads from third-party sources that were generating them online. An average lead was around $10. They were spending around $250,000 a month on sales leads for eighty salespeople.

- An average of $250,000 in leads divided by $10 each = 25,000-26,000 leads a month.

- 25,000-26,000 leads a month divided by 80 agents = approximately **320 leads a month per salesperson**.

- 320 leads a month divided by 20 working days = roughly **16 leads a day** per salesperson.

- 16 leads divided by 8 hours = **2 new leads an hour**. (The numbers vary due to people being sick and not working full days. They are close, but I'm going to round up to make the math easy.)

The end result is that each salesperson got two leads an hour to talk to on the phone, and each lead cost $10. That's $20 an hour or **$160 a day in lead cost per salesperson**. This was what we spent every day per salesperson for them to go to work.

Sales Calls

The lead results broke down like this:

- 50% of sales calls (one call per hour) lasted under five minutes. These calls went nowhere quick.

- 50% of calls lasted more than five minutes. These were prospects.

This meant a salesperson had a shot at closing **one call an hour.** These calls usually lasted about 20-25 minutes.

That left approximately thirty minutes every hour that the salesperson wasn't on the phone. This is called an occupancy rate. It defines how much of their day is occupied actually doing their job.

We were at 50% occupancy ... only half of their day was productive.

Close Rate

Now, as I mentioned earlier, about 20% of the salespeople were closers. They were closing their sales at just under a **20% close rate**. Translated, this means they would get sixteen leads and sell **approximately three sales a day**.

The **bottom 20%** were closing their leads at a **6% close rate**. They got the same sixteen leads and got approximately **one sale a day**.

The balance of our salespeople **had a close rate of** around **12%** and got **two sales a day**.

Everyone was getting the same leads. They had the same opportunity ... and the same sales script. Yet, the close rate was vastly different.

The next area we will discuss is the revenue and cost per sale. Every sale has an average revenue but also has a variable and a fixed cost.

Those costs are made up of:

- The cost of the lead
- The cost of the salesperson
- The overhead of the business

Our revenue and cost per sale on these agents was as follows:

Revenue and Cost Per Sale

Gross revenue per sale was around $2000.

This is the average gross revenue before your hard cost and expenses on an average sale by any given agent.

The company was paid a commission from the product the carrier represented on each sale made for them. This was a percentage of the gross revenue. In this case, 20% commission on gross revenue was the average.

Net revenue (or gross profit) per sale was around **$400**.

That $400 was what we had to work with to pay out all our expenses and then turn a profit.

The next step was to break down what it cost to generate that $400 at a per-person level based on each type of sales agent.

Top Agents

Remember, our top agents averaged three sales a day. This means they generated $400 in net revenue or gross profit three times a day.

Revenue generated: $1200

They got 16 leads at $10 each...so that cost $160 a day

$1200 - $160 = $1040 daily gross profit.

Middle Tier Salespeople

These people represent the majority of our sales force. They average two sales a day. This means they generated $800 in net revenue or gross profit.

Revenue generated: $800

They got 16 leads at $10 each...so that cost $160 a day

$800 - $160 = $640 daily gross profit.

Bottom Agents

Our bottom agents averaged one sale a day. This means they only generated $400 in net revenue or gross profit.

Revenue generated: $400

They got 16 leads at $10 each...so that cost $160 a day

$400 - $160 = $240 daily gross profit.

Now from the top down, it looks like more people drive more sales, which makes more revenue and profits. The top line on the P&L looks better.

Most business owners look at this and think...hey, let's add more salespeople, and we will make even more revenue and grow our way into profitability.

This is exactly what this particular business owner of this company where I was consulting thought. He just couldn't figure out why his profits were not growing. In fact, this company was losing money on 20% of its sales force.

The problem was all those sales in the bottom tier also had both a variable and a fixed operational expense cost attached to them that you couldn't see on the surface.

We were missing vital information in the form of salaries and overall company expenses that hadn't been added to the daily costs.

To finish our individual salesperson P&L, we need to calculate the remaining expenses. This will consist of:

- Salesperson salary and commissions

- OPEX – Company-wide expenses that have to be allocated on a pro-rata basis to each salesperson and then to each sale.

AGENT COST
SALARY AND COMMISSION

Top Salespeople		
	3 Sales Per Day	$300 a day

Middle Salespeople		
	2 Sales Per Day	$200 a day

Bottom Salespeople		
	1 Sales Per Day	$150 a day

So far, so good… But wait! We still have OPEX! (Fixed expenses)

Fixed Expenses

Now this company was in a 25,000-sq-ft facility. They had another small satellite office in Seattle, staffed with four people in accounting and about forty support staff in the main office. This company paid for everyone's health insurance and other benefits. They had an HR department as well. It was a sizable organization.

It ran a fixed overhead of around $400,000 a month.

That $400,000 had to be divided into each salesperson. So, $400,000 divided by eighty salespeople, divided by the working days in the month, equals around $250 a day per salesperson.

Now let's add *that* number to our previous numbers to come up with a net profit per person.

AGENT COST

Top Salespeople

Add the following:

Salary and commission	$300 a day
Lead cost	$160 a day
OPEX	$250 a day
Total daily cost to the company	**$710**
Revenue generated	$1200
	$1200 - $710 = $490
Profit	**$490 per person per day**

Middle Salespeople

Add the following:

Salary and commission	$200 a day
Lead cost	$160 a day
OPEX	$250 a day
Total daily cost to the company	**$610**
Revenue generated	$800
	$800 - $610 = $190
Profit	**$190 per person per day**

Bottom Salespeople

Add the following:

Salary and commission	$150 a day
Lead cost	$160 a day
OPEX	$250 a day
Total daily cost to the company	**$560**
Revenue generated	$400
	$400-$560 = **$160 loss per day**
Loss	**$160 per person per day**

As you can see in the above examples, the bottom-tier sales-people were just straight-up losing money. The middle tier was profitable, and the top tier made a killing.

In fact, while a loss of $160 on a sale doesn't seem like much if you look at the numbers, the bottom 20% of our salespeople represented around sixteen folks. They each made an average of one sale a day for a total of sixteen sales per day, or around eighty sales per week. In fifty-two weeks or a full year, that number was 4160 sales. While it's true they represented around $1.66 million in gross profit; they were actually losing **$166** per sale. Do the math, and this company was losing 4160 X $160 = a loss of $665,600 a year on their bottom-tier crew.

The revenue looked awesome, but the losses added up quick!

It's Time to Go

I was fresh off a plane, consulting with the company. I ran the numbers, took them to the owner, and gave him the news.

I was not just going to fire 20% of his sales force. I was going to fire 40%.

Thirty people would have to go immediately. This would bring the sales team down to fifty salespeople instead of eighty. I was also going to let some of the support staff and a VP go and cut a few other salaries.

The owner was not happy.

I told him that his occupancy rates were at 50%, which meant that his sales team was only working four hours out of an eight-hour day. That was not efficient. We needed to bring that number up to 80%. This would give him more capacity per salesperson, which would increase sales and the close rate. He could buy fewer leads, which would cut overhead. Overall, I assured him his sales would remain the same or go up, with fewer people and a lower OPEX. He would make a LOT more money.

Here is some quick math to better explain the plan.

New Math

The overall close rate for the sales force was around 10.6%. Meaning 10.6% of 25,000-26,000 sales leads were closed.

A 10.6% close rate of 25,000-26,000 leads is roughly 2650 sales a month.

2650 sales x $2000 in revenue = $5.3 million per month in gross revenue and approx. $1 million per month in gross profit before expenses.

Those numbers looked great unless you were talking about the salespeople averaging a $560 sales cost on $400 in gross profit. In that case, you would lose your shirt on every sale.

The first thing we did was fire thirty salespeople and moved the company's sales leads to the salespeople who had the higher closing rate. By eliminating the people with the lower close ratios, we improved our overall close rate from 10.6% to 14.1% while still using the same sales lead cost.

That 3.5% was projected to increase our sales volume from 2650 sales per month to 3525 sales per month. The marketing budget was the same; still, our sales were slated to increase 33%.

Since the cost per sale dropped, the 33% increase in the number of sales made the profit per sale much higher.

Profit went through the roof.

Sales cost went down.

Marketing cost per sale went down.

The salespeople we kept made more money.

Infrastructure cost went down because the company didn't need as much space and overhead.

By rehiring and retraining salespeople over the next six months, we increased sales from around $50 million annually to over $150 million annually.

This was a huge win for this company.

So, what's the moral of this story?

1. More people don't mean more profit.

2. Analyze each individual person on a P&L level to find out if they are making or losing money. Manage your profit margin on every single person in the company.

3. Don't be afraid to make bold cuts. I would rather manage fewer people with less overhead and less infrastructure for the same profit.

That was a lot of math… If you got it … good for you. If not, look at it again, so you understand what I am driving at.

Most importantly, remember, do not manage your company from the top down. You need to look at it from the *bottom up*.

Business Lesson #18... *KNOW YOUR NUMBERS. They are your best friends.*

101

CHAPTER 13

BEING A CEO

"Be the CEO your parents wanted you to marry."
–Unknown

This is my second favorite topic.

There are so many things to talk about when discussing what it means to be a CEO. This will no doubt be a BIG chapter, and I will probably have to break it up into several subchapters … so here we go.

If you are just starting your business, or if you are a young or small company, congratulations! You are probably the CEO! Now let's see if we can give you some tips to make you a better one.

Part of being the CEO is having the vision for your company. We talked about this earlier.

- What do you do?
- Why did you start this company?
- Why is it better?
- Why should people buy from you?

If you have answered those questions, then you are off to a good start. If you haven't, you need to figure out these answers immediately.

The next step we talked about is the numbers.

- Are you running a clear and concise P&L?
- Do you have detailed accounting?
- Do you know your numbers?
- Do you know your margins?

We talked about having a P&L by salesperson, but you can also have a P&L by product!

Sometimes it doesn't make sense to sell a particular product based on the margins versus the time and expense needed to execute after the sale.

The example I use here involves two of my restaurants. One of them is doing around $3 million in revenue; the other is doing less than $1 million. Both locations require the same number of managers. They have the same square footage space, which means the rent is the same. They both have similar marketing expenses. They require the same amount of work to maintain.

The difference is that one of the locations makes $30,000 a month in profit, and the other makes $3000 a month.

At some point, you have to decide if it's worth the same effort to keep the smaller locations open...or if your time is better spent doing something else, like going on vacation or just working less. Sometimes it's just not worth the effort if the overall profit isn't there.

I have another friend in real estate. She sells homes averaging $300,000. She could literally double her income by selling homes worth $600,000 with the same amount of effort.

So … have you thought through what you're selling?

As you go through this exercise, you should know that low-margin products that eat up infrastructure, time, and resources are just not worth it.

Finally, let's talk about people.

Have you decided who you are in the organization?

I know you're the CEO, but are you the Entrepreneur, the Manager, the Salesperson, or the Specialist? Who are you?

Let me ask you another question. I have an app on my phone that my friends and I sit around playing when we are sometimes drinking. It's called "Would You Rather???" It's a game of choices. Sometimes it's two bad choices, and when those come up, it's funny to see what people would rather do! As I am sitting here, I just pulled up the app and went to the first questions … it gave me two options.

Would you rather:

Save the world, and nobody knows it?

Or … Save the world and die in the process?

The app tracks the answers of everyone who plays it. In this question, 60% of the people answered save, and nobody knows it … and 40% apparently needed the glory and will die telling people.

Interesting game.

The question I have for you is this... Would you rather...make $300,000 a year and work all the time ... or make $200,000 a year and do whatever you want? You can go to the mountains, the beach, or spend a month in Europe. Maybe you want to sit on the lake all summer long with your family and kids.

Even Sam Walton, the founder of Wal-Mart, pondered the "Would You Rather???" game. The following was a statement from him in his book Made in America, as he was nearing death:

"This will sound strange to people who know me well, but lately, I've wondered if I should feel bad about having been so wholly commit-ted to Wal-Mart. Was it really worth all the time I spent away from my family? Am I really leaving behind something on earth that I can be proud of having accomplished, or does it somehow lack meaning to me now that I'm facing the ultimate challenge? I could have kicked back and played with the grandchildren, or I could have devoted the latter years of my life to good works."

This is coming from a billionaire — a level of success in bus-iness that none of us will probably ever reach.

It's a time and lifestyle question. What is your time worth to you? What is your life worth to you?

Kids grow up quick ... and nobody says on their death bed, "I'm sure glad I was busy working all the time and not spending time with my kids and family!" What if you knew you only had five or ten years left? What would you do differently? It's the ultimate question in "Would You Rather???"

Now here is the part that is difficult.

Most entrepreneurs and CEOs are control freaks. They need the thrill of building something; they want it; they thrive on it.

If you want to build real value, however, you need to replace yourself. You need to scale your company without you being the main person who gets things done. You need to be the CEO or the owner who hires a CEO. If you want to be able to go out to Park City every winter for a month and ski while your people do all the work, then you need to be able to run your company from your phone and occasionally a laptop. If you want to scale, you need to be replaceable.

Katy runs my seven restaurants. Most of our vendors and patrons think she is the owner of our company. I have walked into my own places and been asked if I know the owner, Katy. People really like her. I love that. Katy takes care of the company, and I reward her appropriately.

From day one, I have always built my companies from the perspective that I don't want to run them. I will oversee them but not be involved in the day-to-day. I am willing to give up part of my income to buy my freedom. Freedom is the most important thing to me.

If you have accomplished this, you are ahead of probably 90% of other small business owners. You have the basis of building a business that has value and that one day you could sell.

Business Lesson #19... *Play the "Would You Rather???" game.*

Vision

Everyone who starts a business has an idea they are convinced they can execute. Sometimes it's the same old, same old business that one-hundred other people have created, and sometimes it's something new. In each of these cases, the owner's vision is crucial.

Here is the problem. We also know that small businesses fail at an alarming rate. Statistics tell us the following about business failures:

- 30% fail in the first year.

- Another 30% fail in year two.

- Another 40% fail by year five.

- **In any given year, only 40% of small businesses make a profit.**

Here is what you need to understand.

1. These businesses didn't fail because they were super profitable, and the owner walked away from all the profit to do something else. They were losing money ... sometimes for a long time.

2. They didn't just lose the startup capital; they also lost money year over year. Those losses wiped out people's savings. They wiped out college funds. They took money from mortgage payments, car payments, and regular bills.

Early on in my restaurant career, I decided to build my first location from scratch. It was near my home and in a Publix parking lot. I thought it was a great location. Another restaurant had been there before me, so some infrastructure was already in place. (By the way, never try putting a new restaurant in a space where another restaurant has just failed. It failed for a reason, and unless you have a national brand or you are a famous chef, you will also fail. That was my rookie mistake.) I spent $250,000 of my savings building that restaurant out the way I wanted it. We opened, and in the first year, I lost $100,000. In the second year, I lost another $100,000. That meant I was down $450,000. It was time to quit. This location was not going to work. I had other locations that were working, and so I decided to close that one.

I ended up selling it to someone else who thought it was a great deal to get a space already built out. They paid me $80,000. Two years after starting, I was down $370,000 in my restaurant locations. That hurt. But I learned. My point is ... businesses fail, and when they do, you will lose a lot more than your startup capital. I was fortunately in a position that losses of that size didn't crush me. But there are a lot of people out there every day getting crushed by businesses, just like what happened to me in this example.

3. It's even worse if the restaurant is a franchise because the franchisor still wants to get paid on phantom revenue for ten years after you close the business!! (I am not a fan of franchises.)

4. Don't forget the personal guarantee you had to sign for when you opened your place. That is a 5-10-year lease. Your landlord still wants to get paid as well. Even after I sold that location, I still had to guarantee the lease payments to the landlord for another three years.

These failures can be devastating.

It kills me to watch them happen to other people. It's even worse when you look at their businesses and ask yourself *what the hell were you thinking??!!!* Either the business model had no chance, or the owner had absolutely no clue. (Failure filter.) Either way, these businesses never stood a chance...

In both of these situations, there is a solution.

1. The owner can figure out they are clueless and get some help.

2. They can pivot their model to something that will work.

3. They can quit and live to fight another day.

What I have learned is that MOST owners will not take the aforementioned advice because of what I told you earlier. Owners are stubborn and don't listen. They think they are always right and get sucked into their vision. Owners swear they can figure it out before the wheels come off the bus. Their personal filter is failing them.

Do NOT get sucked into your vision if it's obvious to EVERYONE but you that it isn't going to work.

I have tried to work with so many people who ask me for advice only to have them argue with me about why I'm wrong, and they are right about their business... The business that is losing money.

Watching someone fail because they are stubborn is very hard on me!

On the off chance that you are going to listen, then really listen.

In other words, if you are currently not succeeding at the level you want to, then you clearly don't have a proper success filter, and that makes most of your decisions wrong.

If you are in this predicament, you need to listen to someone who has had success. You need to find someone who can analyze your business and give you some clear advice on whether you can fix it or if you should close up or pivot to another model.

When it comes to seeking advice, I am not talking about getting it from your relatives or friends. They probably have less of a clue than you.

Find a consultant.

Find a mentor.

Find someone who knows what they are talking about.

Find someone who has been there and done that.

There is no shame in changing business models mid-stream, and there is no shame in failing. Remember that failing is how we learn.

Continuing to throw money away on a losing business does not make you a hero or a martyr. It just makes you broke and stupid. Sometimes the best plan is to walk away before you lose everything.

Let it die. Walk away.

I have owned thirteen restaurants, and only seven of them succeeded. I only have a 53% success rate. Those losses cost me $650,000. But here is the key ... five of the six losses came early on. I learned from those failures, and now our locations are doing well.

Failing and then going on to succeed will put you in an elite club:

Ray Kroc – Started McDonald's at the age of fifty-one. He was a milkshake machine salesperson before that. I'm guessing he wasn't making so much money in milkshake machine sales that he decided to quit.

Steve Jobs – Started Apple Computer but almost ran it into the ground and was fired. Then he started another company that was acquired by Apple years later, and he became the CEO once more.

Henry Ford – Had two other car companies that failed before he succeeded with Ford Motors.

Abraham Lincoln – Was demoted from captain to private during the war before becoming president.

Elvis Presley – After his first performance at the Grand Ole Opry, it went so badly that they fired him, and they asked him not to come back.

Michael Jordan – Was cut from his high school basketball team because he wasn't good enough.

There are so many examples of super successful people failing that I could write a whole book on it. The point is, in each of these examples, the person learned from their mistake.

Michael Jordan didn't quit because he wasn't good enough. He practiced, learned, and got better. Ford didn't keep the same failing car company. He closed it and started another one. Jobs didn't stick with his original plan of closed system computing; he went on to the iPod and the iPhone and changed the world. Presley didn't stick with country and gospel; he pivoted to Rock and Roll.

They failed.

They learned.

They got right back after it and kept going until they succeeded.

If your business isn't working, maybe you should consider their examples.

Business Lesson #20... *Failure isn't the end.* **_IF YOU LEARN_**, *it's the beginning of your next success.*

Omnipresent

If you're going to be an effective CEO, you need to learn to be everywhere all the time.

You cannot be singularly focused.

CEOs cannot be so wrapped up in one area that they are not watching another.

This is why you can't be a specialist and scale your company. You need to pay attention to so many other things that you just don't have time to be doing the actual work of the company.

There is an acronym I love that better illustrates this point: MBWA. It stands for Management By Walking Around.

When I used to work at an office every day, I would constantly wander around. At one company, I carried a golf club around with me. I'm not sure why but I would practice ghost putting all over the office, even though I was really watching people and processes. I was listening to phone conversations and getting a feel for what was going on.

At another company I consulted for in Chicago, I had a small beach ball. The cubicles were low enough that I could see everyone while I was walking around, and I would throw the beach ball to people and ask them questions. Sometimes the beach ball would continue moving through the office from one cubicle to another while I followed along. Again, I was watching, listening, and learning. This is how I kept a pulse on the business.

Today, as I said earlier, I wander around through technology. The apps I use give me real-time information. The weekly P&Ls allow me to study the numbers. In fact, when I took a break from writing this book today, I went through six weekly bill sheets and P&Ls for the restaurants.

Cameras on my phone can look over all the restaurants. I can see the kitchen. I can see how many tickets are hanging on the line. I can see bartenders not paying attention to their customers. I can see managers hanging out in the office instead of being on the floor. I can see customers getting frustrated because nobody is paying attention to them.

When I see this stuff, I start blowing up cell phones. My management team absolutely knows that I may not be looking all the time, but I am always potentially looking.

The joke is that I can see an unhappy customer from one-thousand miles away before they do.

I am everywhere, and you should be, too. Build systems that give you the ability to monitor your operations all the time and from everywhere.

What is Wrong?

I am constantly telling my managers, "Your job is to look around all the time for what is not right."

Remember that old kid's game where you had to find what was wrong with the picture? When you walk into your business in the morning, you should make mental observations about everything you see. When you are wandering around during the day (MBWA), you need to look at your entire operation and what isn't right. (Your business has a proverbial four walls, a floor, and a ceiling. Are you looking at all of them every day?). When you study your bank accounts or P&Ls, you should search for problems. If you catch the problems early enough, then you can avoid them blowing up into real issues later.

One of my best and worst traits is that I can see what's wrong instantly. It's a really weird characteristic. I can find a misspelled word in a marketing brochure or mathematical errors in an Excel spreadsheet quickly. I don't know why, but problems are obvious to me. Now in business, this has served me well ... in my marriage ... NOT SO MUCH!!! :-O

Business Lesson #21... *Look for the problems and fix them every day — all the time. Always look for what's wrong.*

Employees and Vendors

The devil you know is almost always safer than the devil you don't know.

I can't tell you how many times our organizations have gotten rid of an employee or vendor that we thought was marginal, only to hire another one who was the same or worse.

We wasted time and energy retraining someone only to be back in the same position we were trying to get out of.

Most of the time, when this happens, it is caused by the owner's lack of understanding that the employee is not the owner and is never going to look at or treat the business the way the owner does. Try not to be emotional about these decisions. You can spin in circles cycling through people hoping to find perfections that are rarely there.

One of my friends is a relatively new business owner with a restaurant in Florida. He was telling me a story the other day about a manager of his.

One night he walked into the bar, and the first thing he noticed was that the place was lit up like a Christmas tree. He found the manager and asked why the lights weren't dimmed down. The manager told him he hadn't noticed and didn't know where the dimmer switch was.

My friend said he was shocked at the manager's response. He couldn't believe the guy hadn't noticed or thought anything was wrong.

I told him I was shocked that he was shocked!

He shot me a puzzled look and said, "What do you mean?"

I then shared that his manager was an employee, not an owner. Employees don't look at a business with a critical eye. They aren't looking for issues that need fixing. They are focused on the manual task of their job only and waiting to get off work so they can go home. Employees will never look at a business like an owner.

My friend told me that he wanted to fire this employee. I told him that the next person he hired probably wasn't going to be any better.

They are employees. They will never perform at the level you think they should. That's just a fact of business. They are the devil you know. The next person you hire is the devil you don't know.

My rule of thumb is simple.

1. First, we have to decide if the employee's level of output is acceptable based on the level of contribution (what we pay them). In other words, is the employee doing an adequate job … in whatever job they are doing?

2. Are we expecting too much from an employee or vendor?

3. Have a frank conversation in a positive manner to try to get the party in line with where we need them to be.

4. Retrain if necessary.

5. Fire only if we feel that the situation is deteriorating to the point that there is no way to win.

This is also known as the pain of staying versus the pain of leaving.

How painful is it going to be to fire and then rehire and retrain another person that might be the same as the one you want to fire?

Is it more or less painful to retrain the existing employee? Choose the lesser pain… and move on.

CEO Truths

Some final thoughts and truths about CEO life and business.

The world is not designed for you to succeed.

The system is not designed for you to succeed.

They are both designed for you to be average.

America is an amazing country. It is the best country in the world. I bleed red, white, and blue. I served in both the Air Force and the Army. I am all-American.

I can say this, and then in the same breath; tell you that this great country, the home of the American dream, is not designed for you to be anything other than average. I will go one step further and say the world ... the invisible hand ... our government ... society as a whole ... and your employees will actually try and hold you back from achieving great success.

If you think that anything will be easy, you are wrong. If you think the government is here to help you, you are wrong. If you think that people will cheer your success, you are wrong.

You can be average. That is fine.

But as soon as you decide to stick your head up above the crowd and try to do more and succeed more, someone ... and probably a lot of people will try to bring you down.

It will probably be your competition.

It could be someone who just doesn't like you.

It might be an employee you fired who files false accusations against you with some government agency.

It might be a bureaucrat who doesn't think you deserve to succeed.

It could be a naysayer unhappy about everything in life who wants you to suffer as well.

In this day and age of social media, there is no doubt that someone online will try to bring you down for some unknown reason. These people are just unhappy.

Years ago, one of my employees came forward and said they had been sexually harassed.

We immediately went into our protocol. We interviewed everyone who was there. We took a statement from both parties. We followed the guidelines laid out for this particular situation.

In the end, we could not find anyone who could corroborate the incident. In our tight working environment, multiple people were around. We just couldn't find anything.

Even so, we counseled the accused and then changed schedules so the parties would never see each other again. The accuser signed off on a statement that they were happy with the actions we took and the solution we put in place. We put this statement in a file. The accuser never came back to work. They were a "no call, no show" the rest of the week.

Three months later, we received a sexual harassment claim from the state initiated by this employee. The investigator requested all our files on the matter. In this complaint, there were now three incidents. Dates were provided for each incident. When we pulled the payroll records, we saw this person wasn't even working the days the incident supposedly took place. These were clearly false accusations. We had the records to prove it.

We sent everything to the investigator and waited. Six months later, we got a letter requesting personal interviews at our location. We figured that these would be quick chats since we had proved that the individual wasn't even working on the particular days when they claimed they were harassed, and we had the schedules showing that they had been scheduled and never showed up.

When we spoke with the investigator, it became apparent that he was no longer interested in the sexual harassment issue. He was now claiming we'd fired the individual for filing a claim and then straight out told us that we had probably doctored the payroll records to cover everything up. He said he wanted $100,000 for the individual for pain and suffering.

We told him to have a nice day, and he could leave. Then we were forced to hire a law firm to fight the claim. This person was lying. They were filing false claims with the government. Our lawyers told us that the government always believes the accuser. It doesn't matter if you have it on video. The judges will find against you, the evil business owner, and tell you to pay up. We even offered $5000 to settle since everyone knew it was a bogus claim. The investigator said he was recommending a civil lawsuit.

We subsequently had to settle the lawsuit with the EEOC for $20,000. We paid our law firm another $30,000 to fight them. The judge told us that he was shocked the EEOC took the case because it was so weak. However, he said the EEOC doesn't lose. They have all the resources of the government to bankrupt us over time. He told us to settle and walk away. We settled. We were then forced to say we did something we didn't do.

The entire incident, of course, makes me angry. There is no justice in justice. It's just how much money you want to spend to fight.

By the way, as smart as I think I am at this point, my real mistake was not informing my insurance carrier of the incident in the time frame allowed. We were a month late filing the claim because we didn't think the case had any merit, and I didn't take it seriously. Had I done that, they would have handled the case, and I would only be out my deductible of $5000 instead of $50,000. In this case... I learned. I won't make that mistake again!!

Nothing will be fair in business. If you think anything is fair, you will get burned.

You need to stay vigilant.

You need to protect yourself.

You need to always try to figure out how you can get screwed or taken advantage of in any and every deal you do. I go into every negotiation or contract, playing the devil's advocate.

I ALWAYS assume the other party is trying to take advantage of me, and I need to figure out how.

This is especially true when you are dealing with lawyers. Lawyers are your worst enemy. They will write tiny clauses in contracts that they can come back to later to completely take advantage of you and ruin your life. DON'T trust lawyers. They are not your friends.

If you want to succeed in a big way, you are going to have to:

1. Push the limits of what you can and can't do.

2. Never forget that you are building YOUR family's future first.

3. Remember that even your best friend will take advantage of you and your money if it is in their family's best interest. I love my friends, but this is MY future we are dealing with. So, if your best friend will do that, think about what everyone else will do.

4. Watch your ass-ets. Nobody else is.

5. Everyone will have their hand in your pocket. A million companies have the latest and greatest thing you need to buy to make your business better. You don't need 99% of what's peddled. The government will have their hand in your pocket as well. Be very careful and negotiate everything you do. Too many hands will leave you with nothing at the end of the day.

6. Pay yourself first. Martyrs don't succeed... that's why they are martyrs. (Re-read that one.)

7. Just because someone works for a big company doesn't mean they are smarter than you. You would be surprised at how many incompetent billion-dollar company executives there are. The truth is that most of them are only good at playing politics. They aren't really that smart, and most would fail at starting their own business. I see it all the time. They don't have a clue.

8. You don't need to have all the answers, and the truth is you DON'T have them. You need to learn to ask the right questions. This is the key to success. Jack Welch, who is considered the greatest business leader of his generation, was famous for asking questions. If Jack Welch believed in asking questions, you should, too. ALWAYS go in with questions and not answers.

9. One last thought, and I have to throw it in because it is a pet peeve of mine, and I HATE it when I see this happen. DO NOT go to the local franchise show in your town and smell the amazing pretzel smells and drink the amazing smoothies and think that owning their franchise is the answer to your prayers. Those shows are there to suck you in and take your money. Your success rate in most of these ventures is almost ZERO.

There are absolutely some good franchises…but most of the ones you see at the franchise shows are only there to promise you an incredible future and tell you that they have all the answers. Let me repeat. They are just there to take your money and lock you in for ten years… DON'T DO IT.

It may feel like this chapter was more about the negative than the positive. But you need to be prepared for what's real and not uphold a fantasy about owning and running a company. If you don't understand the downside, you are going to constantly be disappointed.

**If you understand and own up to everything
—even the ugly parts—then life will be
that much easier.**

I love owning businesses, but I also understand the downside. So, I can take it in stride when the &^%$ hits the fan. It's just part of the deal.

Business Lesson #22... *Pretending the negative doesn't exist is a recipe for disappointment, depression, and disaster. Understand the deal!!!*

CHAPTER 14

NEGOTIATING—YOU NEED TO BE *RELENTLESS*

"If you can't walk away from a negotiation, then you're not negotiating; you're working out the terms of your enslavement." Unknown

Negotiation is another one of my favorite topics and 50% of the material in my next book. This is a skill that you have, or you don't. Fortunately, you can learn this one. However, it may take a while, and you may have some brutal experiences before you're done learning.

If you don't currently have this skill, you need to find someone who does to help you. Get their help before you run up against someone who is good at it and is negotiating against you. This reminds me of an old saying about "money and experience."

"When a man with money meets a man with experience, the man with the experience will end up with the money, and the man with the money will end up with the experience."

This is so true.

The most powerful negotiating tool you can have at your disposal is also the simplest one to learn, remember and use.

No matter how bad your negotiation is going, if you're stuck, if you can't think fast enough, if you're overwhelmed, or if you're not sure if this is a good deal or not, what I am about to tell you is your get-out-of-jail-free card. It is your saving grace. It buys you time. It puts you back in control. It backs off the other person. This is it, and it's simple... **Just say NO.**

Coincidently this is the topic of one of my next books: *NO*...

Whenever someone makes a first offer, no matter what it is, just say no. First offers are never something a seller or buyer expects to get a yes to anyway.

I don't care how desperate you are; never take a first offer.

Just say no.

One of my friends is selling her house right now. She has a real estate agent who is clearly not on her side. This agent is only interested in getting a commission and doesn't care about my friend.

My friend called me last week and said the agent brought her an offer of $190,000, but after the inspection, they dropped it to $170,000. She said she really needs the money to pay bills and wanted to know what she should do. I told her to just say no, to reply that the price is $190,000.

I could hear the nervousness in her voice as she again told me she needed to sell the house and didn't want to lose the sale. I repeated that she should call them back and say no — tell them that the price of her house is $190,000. I told her to trust me. They were lowballing her because the agent didn't care, and the buyer thought she was desperate.

Her situation reminds me of something I read in a book by Richard Branson whose title I can't remember. He said that if the first offer you make doesn't insult them, it's too high. My friend agreed with me and did what I suggested.

A little while later, she called me back and said they had come up to $180,000 but that it was their final and best offer. I told her to call back and say no. Her counter was $185,000. She repeated again that $180,000 was their best offer.

I said to her, "Look, you're asking me for my advice, and I'm giving it to you. You're already up $10,000. Please do what I'm suggesting, or don't ask me for advice! You will settle on $182,000."

She hung up the phone, and I'm sure she was thinking she was going to kill me when she lost the deal, but she did what I suggested. The next day she called me and told me that she had accepted their offer at $182,000 — $12,000 higher than the first offer and $2000 higher than their best offer.

This is just the way the game is played. The worst that could have happened is they just would have said no. If that had been the case, she still could have accepted their first offer at $170,000. She was willing to take that offer because she was not a negotiator. Fortunately, she called someone who is ... and listened.

Business Lesson #23... *If you're not good at negotiating, find someone who is.*

Walk Away

The second rule of killer negotiating is another one that is easy to say but a bit harder to do ... especially if you are emotionally involved. It comes in three parts:

1. Don't get emotionally involved in any deal.

2. Be prepared to walk away from the deal and play the long game.

3. Everything is negotiable.

We heard that a restaurant was for sale near one of our current locations. We knew that the owner was absent and having a few issues. They were asking $300,000 for the business.

I inquired and got ahold of the financials for the location. As I stated earlier, this is always the first step. As expected, the owner did not have any numbers available and had to figure out how to go get them. This is always the first sign of an inexperienced business owner. They were asking me for $300,000 and did not even have financials ready to look at. Should I assume that they thought I would not care about the numbers? Did they think that I would simply write them a check for $300,000 and say thanks!!! *Blows my mind...*

I finally got the numbers and was not surprised at what I found. The business was a wreck.

Remember what I told you earlier, that most people don't just get up one day and say, "I am making so much money here that

I am going to sell this business and do something else." (Unless someone offers them a LOT of money!).

Labor costs were nearly double what they should have been. This told me the owner wasn't watching and didn't really know what the numbers should have been. The COGS (cost of goods) was 50% higher than it should have been. The manager was being paid nearly double a standard salary for someone running a location of that size. The company was ten years old and going downhill.

I re-ran the numbers based on fixing the obvious issues and figured I could make about $100,000 — considering current sales. I went back and offered $200,000 in a cash and financing deal. They said no, and I walked away.

I heard later that they ended up selling that location to someone else who clearly didn't understand what they were getting into. This was a guy who had come from a corporate background. His newly purchased company got bought out, and he lost his job.

> **About a year later, the broker came back to me and told me that the new owner had decided to sell the location (shocker).**

He was willing to take the $200,000 offer I had made the previous owner. Since I never take the first offer and I knew he was not happy there, I lowered my offer to $100,000. (I was following the mantra of "if your first offer does not insult them; it's too high.") My move clearly insulted him, and he said he would just hire a manager to manage it and keep it.

About six months later, the broker came back to me and said the owner was now willing to take my $100,000 offer for the business. Again, I laughed. Apparently, his manager wasn't working out.

I also found out that he had been hired back to his old company and needed to move. On top of that, his lease was set to expire, and the company wanted him to sign for another five years. This is what I call blood in the streets. It was time to attack.

Since I never take the first offer, and I knew he was out of options, I countered at $0. Yes, I offered him nothing. Instead, I would buy his inventory, pay him his lease deposit back and take over the franchise agreement, which would release him from that eight years of commitment he had left as well.

He was not happy.

What had happened to the $100,000?

His business was doing about $1.2 million in sales annually. It was very profitable. I reminded him that he had no other options, and my deal relieved him of a lot of long-term issues he didn't need.

We went back and forth for a couple of days and settled on $10,000. I paid $10,000 for a business that I had offered $200,000 on two years earlier and $100,000 on one year after that.

I played the long game.

It took over two years.

I was not emotionally attached to this deal.

I always figure, if it's meant to be, it's meant to be, and if I don't get the deal, I will get another one down the road.

I will absolutely not cave on a deal. There will ALWAYS be another good deal out there.

You don't have to have this particular deal right now.

That was three years ago, and once we put our systems in place, that business made well over $200,000 in profit in that time frame — and I basically never go there.

Remember when working on a deal:

1. Never chase a deal.

2. Never take the first offer.

3. Play the long game and walk away if you don't get exactly what you want.

4. Everyone starts WAY higher than what they expect to get, hoping you will negotiate them down a little, so they will still win.

5. Your counter should be ridiculously low.

6. This is NOT the last great deal out there.

7. Find out why the other person is selling what you want to buy and use that information.

8. The other person is willing to sell you a giant pile of garbage for a LOT of money — if you're dumb enough to take it.

Business Lesson #24... *Final thought on walking away. Always remember the winner's curse in negotiating: "Whatever you paid was more than ANYONE else was willing to pay..."*

The Power of Silence

I want to wrap up our negotiation chapter with another very powerful tool you need to learn to use when buying or selling or even when you are just negotiating paperwork like pricing or contracts.

Allow me to break this into two parts.

1. Don't be so quick to talk. A proverb in the bible reads: "Even a fool is thought wise if he keeps silent, and discerning if he holds his tongue." I like to flip that around and simplify it for you: "The less you talk, the smarter you appear. And you have no place else to go but down by talking."

As long as people still assume you're smart, you are in a better position to negotiate.

Remember, your job in any negotiation is to ask questions. Find out what the other party is thinking. Keep them talking, and maybe they will reveal information that you can use.

In my story that I shared earlier, I learned by asking questions. I learned the lease was expiring on the guy I was negotiating with. I found out he had gotten a job and needed to move. I discovered that he still had an eight-year commitment to the franchisor. If he closed his business, that franchisor would still want to get paid the average franchise fees for another eight years. The seller would owe them $320,000. First, I asked questions. Then I used the information he shared with me to get him down to $10,000.

The second part of successfully negotiating is to stick to the rule "the next person to talk loses." This is another subtle human psychology trick you need to understand. People hate silence. This little fact gets even more intense when someone is silent and staring at them at the same time. It makes them uncomfortable, and they feel the need to talk.

Once again, in my example above, after asking all these questions and finding out what was going on, it was my turn to make him an offer. I had already done all the due diligence. I even provided him with financials showing that I had the money ready to go. I had brought my team in to look at everything and interview the employees. We were WAY down the road on this one. The seller knew the deal was going to happen; it was just a matter of how much we were going to do it for. In his mind, this deal was done.

As we sat in the dining room of the restaurant, I knew he would offer it to me for $100,000. We started the negotiations and then chatted for a few minutes before I went silent. I sat there staring at him for about a minute ... and then told him that I couldn't pay $100,000 for the place and that I would offer him $0. You remember the rest of the pitch: I would take over operations and release him from the lease and the franchise agreement. He could walk away.

After I said my piece, I just stared at him. He did not respond right away. I think he was shocked. Before we sat down, he had been ready to negotiate something, but he was not ready for my terms. The rule here is that the next person to speak loses the dominant position in the negotiation. So, we just stared at each other.

I was not going to say anything else, and he was beginning to figure that out as well. Finally, he said he just couldn't do the deal and walk away with nothing.

But he had spoken first and was now in the weaker position. He had this deal done in his mind and didn't think there was any way it wasn't going to close. Hearing my terms left him stunned. I told him that was the best I could do, and I would walk away from it if he didn't take it. We sat there for another thirty minutes talking before we finally agreed to $10,000 plus about $8000 in inventory and $9000 for the lease deposit. I would write him a check for $27,000, and he could move on. In return, I got a million-dollar business.

And here's my final note. If you find yourself in this situation, be prepared for the person you're talking to, to also know what I'm telling you here. If they are probing you for information, they are probably looking for your weak spot.

That's OK. Don't fold. And don't speak!

Business Lesson #25... *The first person to speak after an offer loses. Don't be a loser!!!*

CHAPTER 15

MONEY

"Business is the art of extracting money from another man's pocket without resorting to violence." –Max Amsterdam

Let's be honest... Unless you're a saint, the reason you started your business and the reason you want to grow it is money. You want to make lots of money. You believe that being in your own business is the best way to make lots of money, and I agree with you. Unless, of course, you're a Wall Street guy, or investment banker ... or maybe a venture capitalist. Those people make a lot of money.

Personally, I didn't have that option. And if you're reading this book, I doubt you have that option either.

So, let's talk about money.

Money is a means to an end.
It's paper.
It's also a scorecard.

It measures your success or failure in your business.

If you make a bunch of it, you are considered successful. If you lose it, you're a failure. (For now. Unless you learn, then it's a steppingstone. Don't forget this part.)

Money first becomes important to us because it's a way to pay the bills. If you're having success, it becomes a way to accumulate things that you've always wanted but couldn't afford. Next, it becomes something you save for a future date, so you won't need to go make it anymore when you're older. If you make enough, it becomes something you can give away for a greater cause that you care about. Lastly, it becomes something you can pass on to your children to give them a head start in life.

Each of these steps is an evolution in the making of money. Your progress through these steps depends on you. If you have passed the paying-the-bills stage and are starting to accumulate things, your progression will depend on how much you think is enough. How many cars do you need and how many houses are enough? If you are in the saving mode, you will need to determine the lifestyle you want in the future, so you can figure out how much money you need to save to reach that goal.

Stuff

Some people never stop accumulating stuff. They are "things rich" and "security poor." They have all the toys. (By the way, toys are depreciating assets… They burn cash.)

I used to have so many toys. I had a lake house with a boat and two WaveRunners, a plane I kept down at the airport, a beach place, a 10,000-sq-ft main house with seven fireplaces, a pool, two hot tubs, a gym, and a theater. There was the Mercedes SL600 twin-turbo convertible, a BMW 650i, a Hummer, and two motorcycles. It was ridiculous.

I used to say, "The more stuff you have, the more stuff that breaks, the more stuff you have to fix, the more money you throw out the window every month."

I couldn't use all those toys, so most of the time, the batteries would just go dead. The grass would need to be cut at the houses. Plumbing would leak in the houses and make huge messes while I was gone for six months in the off-season. The insurance was ridiculous. I blew through a lot of money on toys.

I had made a bunch of money and achieved every financial dream I'd ever had, and much like most people who make a lot of money quickly, I needed to acquire every material possession I'd ever wanted ... all at the same time. So, I did.

I lost several million dollars just in the lost value and upkeep on all that stuff. I burned through money monthly at a rapid clip.

People in the accumulation phase, much like I was, are fine as long as the money keeps coming in. If it stops, they tend to lose it all.

Years earlier, I remember asking my friend, a professional baseball player, why so many athletes go broke after they make huge sums of money. We were riding down the road one day on our way to the nursery to buy some plants for his yard. His baseball team was about to make it to the World Series. They had just gone up to play Minnesota in the playoffs. I will never forget what he told me that day in the truck. It went something like this.

"Brian, I pay cash for my cars and my house. I don't invest in anything but T-bills and bonds. I don't make a great return, but I always know where my money is and that it will be there when I need it. I don't need to get a good return on my money; I don't need the next great amazing investment. I make a LOT of money playing ball and have enough in the bank to last a lifetime. There is no need for me to risk it and potentially lose it. The number one mistake most players make is thinking that the money will go on forever."

He told me he and his team went to Minnesota for the play-offs, and it was really cold. A bunch of the players all went out and bought mink coats to wear while they were there. They spent thousands of dollars on a coat. He said, "I went to Kmart and bought a down jacket for fifty dollars." He didn't need a mink coat, so he didn't buy one.

The second biggest mistake these athletes make is thinking that because they make a lot of money, they are somehow now a financial genius.

They have an attitude of *I'm a millionaire now, so I must be a financial genius, and soon I will be a billionaire.*

They invest in stupid things, and high-risk ventures pitched to them by people with "experience." (Remember what I said about people with money meeting people with experience. "The people with experience end up with the money, and the people with money end up with the experience.") These two things are the root cause of many high-income athletes losing all their money.

But these principles don't just apply to pro athletes; they apply to any businessperson. Just because you're a genius at soft-ware, at being a doctor, or at owning a print shop, or any other business that does millions in sales, that does not make you a financial wizard. Remember who you are, then do what you do best and let other professionals do what they do best.

Business Lesson #26... *Be careful buying stuff, and remember it's a depreciating asset. The more you buy, the faster it drops in value, and you can never get back what you spent. Your stuff will all eventually be junk anyway.*

Savings

This is my favorite of all the money stages, what I refer to as my "McDonald's Safety Net." I talk about this in my first book but will reiterate it here.

At some point in your life, you need to decide what your minimum level of living is and what you can live with if the wheels come off the bus. In other words, if you lost your primary source of income and couldn't get it back, how much money would you need to have saved or invested, so if you had to, you could work at McDonald's and still maintain your lifestyle?

I know that sounds like an odd question, but this is the thought that rolled through my mind back in 1999 when I sold my first company.

I got cash, stock, and a job from that sale. There was enough cash to pay off all my personal debt and my house. I remembered my lesson from my friend years ago about being safe with your money, so I went down to the bank and told the banker I was there to pay the house off.

Incredulously, he argued with me about what I was about to do. It was January of 2000. The stock market was in a full bubble state. Stocks were climbing like crazy.

The banker told me that I should take my money and invest it in the stock market. The dot-com boom was making everyone millionaires. I told that banker about my friend and his story about protecting your future. The banker didn't want to hear it.

It took me twenty minutes to convince him to pay off the mortgage. I was officially in what I thought of as my McDonald's safety net. I was not rich. I did not have a Mercedes or a mansion. I had a $300,000 house and a couple of nice cars. But they were paid for. I had no bills and no debt, and so I needed very little money to live on. I was happy with that lifestyle at the time because I was safe. And there is a lot to be said for safe.

Three months later, in March of 2000, the bubble burst. Dot-com stocks dropped up to 90%. If I had listened to that banker, I would have lost everything, and I still would have had all my debt. Not only that, but I would have wasted the last years of my life building and selling a business, only to watch it all go away in a couple of days from a "SMART" investment. I have never forgotten that lesson.

Business Lesson #27... *After the bills are paid, safety should be your number one concern before stuff. Stuff should be the reward for the safety net, not the reward for making the money in the first place.*

Giving It Away and the Kids

**If you are in the accumulation phase,
you should also be thinking about your legacy.**

My friend, an author and businessman out of Park City, sat me down one day a few years ago at lunch and asked me what I was going to do next. I told him I didn't know, then shrugged and said, "Maybe I'll start another business."

This is another one of those conversations you walk away from and have to think about.

Next, he asked me a simple question... "Why?" I shrugged again. He pressed, "Do you need the money?" I told him, "No," and he said again, "Then why?"

I couldn't answer his question then. I was in flux with my life at fifty years old and didn't know what I wanted to do when I grew up.

We were sitting at an outside table at a Starbucks in Park City in the winter. It was cold, and we were all bundled up in our ski clothes. In between bites of his sandwich, my friend looked up at me and asked, "Brian, do you have a passion in life?" I thought about it for a minute, and it struck me that I didn't.

I had lost all my earlier-in-life drive to succeed. I had lost the drive I'd had that made me need to beat out everyone else.

I didn't need to be a billionaire.

I didn't need any more houses or cars.

As another friend once told me: "A steak can only be so good, and you can't eat it every day. A bed is only so soft, and you can only travel so much."

I was satisfied and didn't need to work anymore. I had no drive and passion anymore.

My friend then said, "Brian, you need to find a passion. You made the money; now you need something that is lasting and leaves a legacy. You need to have a purpose in life."

Money can provide those things in the sense that you can give it away to causes you care about. It can also give you the freedom and time to give yourself away to charities or events to help people. Maybe you will be able to help your children start their own business, help them buy their first house, or leave them millions of dollars in the bank when you're gone. Maybe it can even give you a platform to write a book. Like the book you're reading, or the one I wrote before this one about life lessons for my kids.

It has taken me five years to write these two books. But I know they will live on past me. My kids and grandkids will always have them so they can read about their dad and grandfather. They will be able to understand the way I thought and why I did what I did in my life. That was part of my passion that I needed to find.

Business Lesson #28... *Find your passion. Today, it may be paying the bills. Tomorrow, it may be buying things or saving money to give yourself security. But eventually, if you're successful, you will want a legacy. What will yours be?*

Money in Business

Before we move on to the next chapter, let's discuss a few money concepts that concern your business.

Here is the number one rule... Cash is king.

I tell my management teams all the time that we have another number one rule, and it's the golden rule...

But it's not the golden rule most people know. My rule has nothing to do with how you treat others.

It is this:

He Who Holds the Gold...Rules.

I mean that if you are the buyer in any transaction, **you hold the gold**. The other person wants it, and that makes you the king. You set the rules. You decide if and when you will release that money. It's 100% your call right up until you hand it over. Then you are no longer the king, and you are at the other person's mercy. Holding the money is your negotiation tool. This is how you swing things in your favor. This is your leverage as long as you hold it.

Business Lesson #29... *He who* **HOLDS** *the gold rules. When you pay someone, they hold the gold!!*

Cash is King. Period.

Your cash position determines your security if things go sideways. Cash gives you the ability to pay bills if you have a temporary glitch in revenue. Having cash is more important than paying off debt in the beginning of operating your business.

> **Given the choice of having $100,000 in cash in the bank and long-term debt of $100,000, or zero cash and zero debt, I will take having the cash and the debt every time.**

You can't go to the grocery store and tell the cashier, "Alright! So, I would like to buy these groceries, but I didn't get that check I was expecting today, so I don't have any cash until next week. But remember, I don't have any debt either, so I'm good for it."

Having no cash means no groceries for you!!

This rule doesn't just apply to small businesses, either.

Debt is not always bad. In September of 2019, Apple computer had $211 billion in cash on hand. At the same time, they raised $7 billion selling bonds in the public market. Here's the question: why would Apple borrow $7 billion when they already had $211 billion in cash?

Apple knew that the cash was more important than the debt. They also knew that they could use the borrowed money to invest in things that would generate a greater return than the 2.5% interest they were paying. In Apple's case, they used the money to buy back stock at roughly $225 a share. Today that stock sits at just over $300 a share. They have gained $75 per share in eight months. That is a 33% increase in eight months versus 2.5% interest over that same timeframe. The debt was good.

In the case of a small business, you never want to strap yourself down with no cash. This causes unneeded stress if the next sale is delayed or the next check is another week out. You should always have available cash to get through a tough situation.

We are seeing people struggle with keeping cash in the coffers right now in America. As I am writing this, we are six months into the great American shutdown due to the coronavirus and are at an unprecedented time in American history.

Estimates are that 20-30% or more of small businesses are going to fail in the next six months. In our mixed-use development alone, three of ten restaurants have shut down. I am in the process of picking up one of these locations right now for five cents on the dollar of what they paid to open it one year ago. I can do this because I have the cash the seller needs. I have the gold.

I will reopen this location, and it will do over a million in sales in the next year.

These businesses that are failing were strapped for cash and running on the bleeding edge of profitability before corona. They set themselves up for failure. This kind of extreme situation may never happen again, but nevertheless, millions of people will lose their life savings and be out of business because they weren't prepared for any problem, let alone one of this magnitude. The coronavirus accelerated the shutdown of many businesses that would have shut down anyway at some point.

Business Lesson #30... *Cash is king.*

Pay Yourself First

The same principle I just talked about in business also applies to you personally.

You need to pay yourself.

You need to set yourself up personally for any downtimes as well.

This isn't always easy, but you need to do it.

I have heard so many stories about people who have sunk everything into their business. They've felt like martyrs for the company. They've thought *if I just sacrifice everything, it will be all right one day.* These are also the people who always tell the story of some guy who risked it all, and it worked out.

I hear stories like that all the time. It's because they make for awesome entertainment. Nobody sits around talking about everyone who failed. But they do, and when these people fail, they lose everything. Business is tough, so pay yourself first ... even if it's just a little bit.

Business Lesson #31... *Pay yourself. You have no idea what may happen, and if you need it and can't work, you will be glad you have the money.*

CHAPTER 16

TO SELL OR NOT TO SELL

*"I look at building business as a creative process
that I enjoy." –Chad Hurley*

Selling is another of my favorite topics.

Understand going into this chapter that I am a "build and sell" guy. I'm not here for forever. I am here to start something, scale it, and sell it.

The building part is the exciting part. Building is the front side of the bell curve of your business. I will never come into work every day and manage a stagnant company — that is what we call the backside of the bell curve when launching a company. I can hire someone else to do that, or I can sell it and do something exciting again.

As I told you, the first company I sold was an insurance call center. It set the stage for my buy and sell mantra. I sold it to a venture capital company. After a few name changes, it went public under the name Connecture. It has since gone back to private. Connecture is a very large player in the Medicare space.

The second company I sold was an internet marketing company called Monetizeit. We were an online middleman for people who wanted to sell things online and focused primarily on the subprime credit markets. This was before the subprime crash and subsequent legislation to control this industry.

Here is how it worked. The market had lots of companies that wanted to get people signed up for high-interest credit cards. So, they had a product. There were also lots of companies, or in some cases, individuals who had email marketing lists that could mass market to a lot of people really quickly. For argument's sake, let's say there was an email list of one-hundred million emails. We sat in the middle as a "pay for performance" online marketing company.

People with products would come to us and ask us to get applications filled out for their credit cards. They would offer to pay us a flat amount per application, usually between $5 and $20 per application.

We would then build them an online website and all the online marketing and tracking materials to go with it. We would also set up the online application process and handle the transactions on our servers.

Then we would go out into the market and find online marketing people who needed products to sell, and we would offer our products to them at anywhere between $2 and $10. They would only get paid if they had a completed application. That's because the credit card company would only pay *us* for a filled-out application. This is called "pay for performance" marketing, meaning there was no cost unless a transaction happened. These marketers would send out one-hundred million emails a day with our offers.

We literally sat in the middle with no skin in the game except for our internal team, who built everything and would collect, on average, around $8 a transaction at approximately 10,000 transactions a day.

We sold this company three and a half years later, after being approached by a private equity firm out of Chicago.

They were standing on our front doorstep one day when my partners and I came to work. They wanted to talk to us about buying the company.

Sixty days later, we closed the deal for around $60 million in cash, an eight-figure earnout, and another eight figures in stock. It was crazy!! Later down the line, this firm combined our company with three other companies they had purchased and put them back up for sale for $350 million.

The third company I sold was another online insurance agency. We were running it simultaneously with a marketing company. After the big sale, I was pretty much done working, so I looked for a buyer. It took me another year and a half before I found one. The buyer was another venture capital company out of Silicon Valley. They combined it with one of their portfolio companies. Today, that company is called Get Insured. They run several state health insurance exchanges and operate an online insurance platform.

The next company I started was another insurance marketing and insurance software company. I actually let that one go right before it was sold off. I was there less than a year and decided

TO SELL OR NOT TO SELL

that I just wasn't interested in being in the space anymore. It was sold to a very large call center company out of India.

Since then, I have done a fair amount of consulting and now own a chain of restaurants. I currently have seven operational restaurant locations, with two more under construction. The goal is to get them to about $15 million in revenue, and then guess what I will do????

Three Phases

There are three phases to a business.

1. The startup

2. The management

3. The sale.

Phase one and three are the most exciting. When you are in these phases, it is all about making the right decisions, figuring out how to scale, and setting up the management systems.

Once you do that and take your company to a certain level, you need a good manager to keep it going. This is when you get into all the stuff I don't like dealing with: the legal, administration, and governmental. These areas are both boring and risky. When we get to this phase, I am ready to exit.

I also believe every business has a life cycle. It grows. It levels out, and then it either declines or is forced to begin the slow change of adapting to the changing markets. I would rather sell when a business is growing or leveled out. Once you get into

TO SELL OR NOT TO SELL

changing markets, you stand the chance of making the wrong decisions, and your value decreases.

I remember when we sold Monetizit. The five partners were sitting in a room, looking at the offer. Our senior partner said. "OK, guys, we have to be alright with this offer forever. We can't look back if it takes off and think we should have waited. Nobody can see the future."

We all talked about it briefly, and every one of us agreed that it was a good offer, and we should take it. So, we sold the company.

The year we sold it, we did $32 million in revenue. The year after we sold it, it did $60 million in revenue. We were living the exact thing we had talked about.

I remember sitting around with my former partners and having a drink one day after the new buyers had had the $60-million-sales year. We got to talking about it, and I thought *damn...we sold too early. We could have made double!*

But we had to stop ourselves because we had agreed that we would be happy with what we got. So, we said cheers to our good fortune and moved on.

The following year the sub-prime credit market crashed. The government stepped in and hyper-regulated the industry. The entire business model fell apart, and sales dropped from $60 million to around $10 million. The company was in trouble.

Within two years, the private equity firm sold all four companies for $10 million—ten cents on the dollar of what they paid.

Once again, my former partners and I were sitting around having a drink. This time we thought... *THANK GOD we sold when we did!!!*

You never know when someone, something, or the government will step in and destroy what you have spent a lifetime building.

Another example of this conundrum and a different side to the pandemic and a government shutdown has to do with business offers I have made this year.

I made offers on two businesses in February of this year. Both offers were turned down because the seller wanted more money. Just today, one of them called me back and said they would take my offer. I didn't mean to, but I laughed. I then offered thirty cents on the dollar of my original offer. They said no. I told them to call me back when they were interested.

I live by my golden rule of he who holds the gold rules.

I bet that company wishes they had sold to me when we were negotiating over pennies on the dollar. Today they have nothing. We will see what happens... The negotiation may get another jump start.

Business Lesson #32... *If you decide to sell, try not to negotiate yourself out of a deal. Be happy with what you get, and don't ever look back. You have no idea what the future holds.*

Multiples

Generally speaking, when you sell your company, you are offering multiples of EBITDA (Earnings Before Interest, Taxes, Depreciation, and Amortization). Your price can be as little as 1X to 10X or more. The multiple depends on a lot of things:

1. How many locations do you have? The more you have, the more diversified you are, and the less the long-term risk is of the entire operation going under.

2. The depth of your client base. A business with one thousand clients is far more valuable than a business with ten. If a business with ten loses one client, the business loses 10% of its revenue and maybe 25% of its profit and value. The risk is far greater than a business with one thousand clients. That business can lose one client, and nobody notices. It has depth, and depth is worth more money.

3. Is the business reliant on a single individual? If it is, you are Joe, the plumber, and you have very little value when you leave.

4. Is the business in an industry that allows it to grow? People don't like to buy businesses that can't grow. Unless all the buyer wants is a job, why would they spend the money to buy it when the point is to increase in value?

5. Does the business have recurring revenue? A business with one hundred clients paying $500 a month in recur-

ring revenue is far more valuable than a business that has to replace its customers every time a job is done. Think about it like this. Would you rather have a business that does $100,000 a month selling TVs or $100,000 a month selling toilet paper? How often is your customer going to buy a TV? How often is your customer going to buy toilet paper? I think you know the answer.

6. Does your business have a recognizable brand? Brands sell. This is why people buy franchises. The brand brings customers in without you having to create the market. Buyers love brands.

All of these points take us back to one central question: What is the value proposition of your business? Put another way, what value do you place on it? Answering this question is tricky. It's also super dependent on the buyer.

Strategic buyers are willing to pay more for your company. They are buying it for the purpose of combining it with their brand to increase their overall value. They can accomplish this if they can buy you out for a lower multiple than what they are currently worth. This means the day they close, whatever they paid you goes up in value on day one.

As an example:

Last year a public restaurant company bought a chain of restaurants here in the Atlanta area. The company was doing about $120 million in sales, with profits of around $32 million. The seller was paid $320 million for the chain. That is a 10X multiple and very high!

Why would this public company buy them for so much?

The answer is simple.

The public company was trading at a 20X multiple on Wall Street. That means their stock price was based on twenty times their EBITDA. They only paid *10X* of EBITDA for the restaurant chain. This means the $32 million in profit the new acquisitions brought to the table would be worth the same 20X multiple the public company was currently valued at.

So, the day they closed the sale, the $320 million they paid was worth $640 million on their balance sheet. *They made a $320-million profit in one day.* I would say that is a pretty good deal. It was a strategic investment and worth more than what it would be worth to someone simply buying the restaurant chain for themselves.

I look at multiple earnings as "the ability to collect future profits that don't yet exist and might not ever exist," at a tax rate that is lower than if I earn it out over the same time frame.

If my company makes $1,000,000 a year, I pay taxes at about 40%. Meaning I net $600,000 a year after taxes. In five years, I net $3,000,000.

If I get a 5X multiple on that EBITDA, I will sell the company for $5,000,000. My tax rate in Georgia would be 15% capital gains and 6% state for a total of 21%. I would clear almost $4 million on the sale. That is one million more than I would net over the next five years if I kept the company and kept it working. Broken down, that's basically 6.5 years of future profit that I can collect today. *And* I don't have to work for it, as well as I have no more risk.

Then there is the option of investing that $4 million you have today in a tax-free municipal bond and earning another 3% triple tax-free every year. This would earn you another $120,000 a year in tax-free income. Overall, you have made five years of income in advance and will still make an additional $120,000 a year in interest. All with no risk.

Business Lesson #33... *If you can make future profits with no risk ... do it.*

What's Next

I started my landscaping company when I was twenty-one years old. By the time I was twenty-seven, I had built a small company that was semi self-sufficient. This was the first time I had thought about selling my company. I contacted a business broker I found in the Yellow Pages and met with him about representing me in the sale.

The business broker asked me about my numbers. I told him I was doing maybe $800,000 in sales and making about $150,000 a year in profit. He asked me why I wanted to sell. I told him it would be nice to get a big chunk of money, and I was tired of running the company. I was bored.

He looked at me for a minute and said, "What are you going to do next?" I asked him what he meant. He said that even If he could get me $500,000, after taxes, I would probably net $400,000. "How long do you think you can live on $400,000?" he questioned. "What skills do you have to move into another industry — because you will be locked out of this one for years to come. What are you going to do next to feed your family?" He paused and gave me a hard look, then said, "Because $400,000 is not enough."

I hadn't thought about that question before.

I had no education and no skills that I knew of.
And I had no idea what I would do next.
I asked, "What are my options?"

He told me that he thought I could franchise my company. I could still use my knowledge to help other people succeed, but I wouldn't have to be involved in the day-to-day landscaping while still making a good living. He would set the entire thing up for $25,000.

It sounded like a great idea. However, I told him that if he thought it was such a great idea, he should waive his fee, and I would take him on as a partner instead. He would make far more money in the long run if it worked. I was a bit surprised when he agreed! So, we launched our company and, within a year, had seven franchises in the Atlanta area.

Before you decide to sell, ask yourself, *what am I going to do next?* If you have an answer, then, by all means, sell the company and do something else exciting. But hey, that's just my opinion.

Business Lesson #34... *If you're thinking of selling, what are you going to do next?*

CHAPTER 17

BORROWING SOMEONE ELSE'S FILTER

*"Develop success from failures. Discouragement
and failure are two of the surest steppingstones to
success." –Dale Carnegie*

The toughest part about writing this book is tackling and trying to centralize the infinite possibilities that are out there in all of the different kinds of businesses.

Every business has a different set of struggles and a different set of circumstances.

Every business has a different owner with a different mindset.

As I set out to write this book, I had this crazy idea that I would be able to provide a lot of specific answers to specific questions. I have worked with so many people on their small businesses that I figured a book would help me lay out the answer to a lot of commons struggles I have seen. What I learned along the way was that it's impossible to answer every question because there are too many variables.

Instead, this book ended up being more general in nature, yet more high level than I anticipated.

While I do subscribe to the theory that if you know how to run a business, then you pretty much know how to run any business (within reason), the ability to run that business is actually based on your own filter.

Your chances of success hinge on how you take in, perceive, and act on information. And your success is based on your personal filter.

It's based on your ability to ask the right questions and find the right answers. It's based on your ability to understand who you are and where you belong in your business, as well as your willingness to understand that maybe you're not in the right place in the organization. That's critical. So is your willingness to find someone who can fill what you lack in your role. The challenge lies in the underlying issue of YOU.

If your filter is not up to par, if your ability to ask pointed questions is not developed yet, you need to bring someone else in to help you. You need to find someone who has the experience you require to make good decisions—someone whose filter you can borrow until you can develop your own. Sometimes you just need to understand that you may not be able to make the right decision at a particular time. That's OK. Don't let the fact that you need to learn a little more hold you back.

I Have a Tattoo

In 2003, I had six partners who owned two different companies. I was the senior partner on the insurance side, and I had another partner, Steve, who was the senior partner on the internet side. The insurance company had been around for several years and hadn't made much of a profit, and we had just started the internet company nine months earlier.

Steve had come from another internet company he had started, and he had made millions of dollars. When we launched this new company, we made a deal. Steve would put up $450,000 of his money, and both companies would guarantee the debt back to Steve. Whichever company made money first would pay him back before we would do any distributions.

> **Steve had already been super successful in his last company, so I thought this was a good deal, and we launched.**

Nine months later, our accountant barged into my office and shut the door. I asked him what was up, and he told me that the internet company had lost about $400,000 in the last nine months. He told me that I needed to shut it down before it bankrupted the insurance company. In his words: it was a dead loser.

I went home that night and talked to my wife about the conversation. The next morning, when we were out running, we talked about it again. I told her I just wanted out. I didn't want to guarantee all that debt. It was killing us.

Later that day, Steve came into my office to talk to me about one of the other partners on the internet side who owned 50% of that company. He wanted out and had lost faith in what Steve was doing. He was ready for us to buy back the servers from them. Steve told me we could buy the servers for $66,000, and then we would own the whole company and not just half. He'd put up the money and add it to the debt.

Now, remember, I'd just been talking to my wife that morning and wanted out. But there was Steve telling me we were going to add another $66,000 to the already $450,000 in debt I owed. I felt sick. I told Steve that I didn't think it was a good idea. We had not generated any revenue and had already spent $400,000. I shared the conversation our accountant had had with me the previous day. I was scared.

He told me the internet was like the lottery. You have to keep going after it until you hit a deal, and then it just gushes out money. I told him yes, I could understand that analogy, but we hadn't generated any money in nine months... NONE! And I now owed $516,000.

Steve looked at me and said, "Brian, I will make you a one-time offer. You give me my equity back. I will give you your equity back, and we will walk away as friends, but you need to decide right now."

I sat there staring at Steve for what felt like two solid minutes. I was sweating. The ping pong ball in my head was going back and forth...*do I stay in, or do I get out?* I knew Steve had had tremendous success in the past, and I knew that I hadn't yet made as much money as he had.

I had to decide right then if I was going to trust my decision-making skills or his. My personal filter for critical thinking or Steve's. I finally looked at him and said, "OK, Steve ... **I'm in...**"

I trusted him more than me at this point, and I borrowed his success filter thinking to make that decision.

He gave one firm nod of his head and said, "Good, but I don't ever want to have this conversation again." Then he got up and left my office.

Thirty days later, just like Steve had said, we hit our first deal. Money started rolling in. We did $6 million in revenue that year, paid Steve back all his money, and made a nice profit. The next year we did over $20 million in revenue, and that was the first year I made over a million dollars in one year. The next year we did over $30 million in revenue and got an offer to buy us out from a private equity firm for around $60 million in cash.

My entire life changed in those two years. Everything I have today financially came from that one decision. That day I told Steve, **"I'm in**," my children's lives changed, my grandchildren's lives changed. It was monumental. Today, I have a tattoo on my right shoulder that says, **"I'm IN**," to remind me of that conversation and that day.

It scares me today just thinking about what would have happened if I had trusted my judgment instead of Steve's ... If I had used my success filter instead of his.

In Summary

Before you think that what I told you is a bunch of gobbledygook, I want you to consider a large corporation.

It has a CEO. That CEO oversees the day-to-day operations. But that CEO also has a board of directors that he or she reports to. The board of directors is made up of people in different industries and with different experiences. Their jobs are to provide different perspectives from different backgrounds to the CEO.

They all have different filters. They see and perceive information differently. Their jobs are to advise the CEO on how they would handle things based on what their experience has shown them. They are essentially allowing the CEO to borrow their filters to make better decisions at a faster rate and with a more robust and quicker learning curve.

Consider this as it relates to your business. If billion-dollar companies think it's important that their CEOs have a board of directors to help them manage the company, why wouldn't you want to have at least someone help you in your small business?

Granted, most small businesses don't have the money or resources to create an effective board of directors, but doesn't it make sense to at least find someone else who can help advise you on your company and your future?

Do you really think that you are better at running your company than Apple, Microsoft, or any other massive profitable company that uses a board of directors?

I hope this book helped, if even only in a small way.

Like anything else, if you found one or two nuggets here that you can use to move your business forward, then it was worth the time to read it, and I will feel like I have accomplished my goal.

Last Business Lesson #35... *If your filter is not where it should be, find someone who has the experience and the filter to help you get to the next level ... and use them.*

For those of you who made it to the end of the book and didn't notice, there are only 35 lessons spelled out here.

Bonus Business Lesson #36... *Always read to the end of the contract including the fine print — there might be something you miss.*

Bonus Business Lesson #37... *Don't chase the advice of billionaires. They are so far out of the realm of what you are doing... Their advice probably won't help you. I would rather learn from someone who has succeeded at what I'm doing... Their advice is much more relevant to my daily struggles.*

CHAPTER 18

BUSINESS LESSONS' SUMMARY

"Far and away the best prize that life offers is the
chance to work hard at work worth doing."
—Theodore Roosevelt

In each one of my books, I like to include a final recap chapter detailing all the lessons that I have shared. This gives you a centralized place to go to get the gist of the chapters again without needing to leaf or scroll through the book to find the phrase you are looking for.

I hope you keep these lessons at the forefront of your mind, that you find them helpful in all your future endeavors and that you find much success in your business in the years to come.

PREFACE

Business Lesson #1... *Be careful what you allow in your brain. It will affect everything in your life.*

Business Lesson #2... *Be honest about your situation and your personal filter. If you do not have a success filter, you need to find someone who does and allow them to help you. The only thing standing between you and success in this situation is your ego. Your ego will take you down a dark path if you let it. The truly unfortunate part here is that if you do not have a success filter, you will probably not make the right decision to allow someone to help you, and your failure filter will continue to evolve just like it has in the past.*

CHAPTER 1: A FEW QUESTIONS

Business Lesson #3... *You need to start by being honest about what you have. Are you self-employed? Is that what you want? Don't fool yourself into thinking you have more than you do. You can't grow if you can't be honest with yourself.*

Business Lesson #4... *If you want to own a business and build value, don't be Joe.*

CHAPTER 2: SELF-EMPLOYED VS. BUSINESS OWNER— WHAT ARE YOU?

Business Lesson #5... *Decide what you want to be: self-employed or a business owner. Making that decision is the first step toward how you are going to structure your company moving forward and build your future.*

CHAPTER 3: OK, YOU'RE IN BUSINESS—NOW, WHO ARE YOU?

Business Lesson #6... *Figure out who you are at your core. Don't focus on the tasks you are performing now. Don't let your ego fool you into thinking you are something that you are not. You have to be brutally honest, or your growth will stagnate.*

CHAPTER 4: TWO EXAMPLES OF SPECIALISTS WHO THINK THEY ARE ENTREPRENEURS

Business Lesson #7... *Get your house in order. There are a lot of things you need to have in place to protect you and your business before you begin. If you don't know what they are, find someone who does know. The two biggest protections to put in place and where you need to be informed are having the right insurance and understanding the government regulations around your business and employees. Do not skip these, and don't ever mess with government regulations. You cannot win against them. Ever.*

Business Lesson #8... *PLEASE understand that if you aren't succeeding in what you're doing, you probably have a strong failure filter that is making the wrong decisions for you about what you should be doing. You are fighting an uphill battle that you probably will not win.*

CHAPTER 5: THE PROBLEM WITH SALESPEOPLE AND MANAGERS

Business Lesson #9... *Salespeople generally don't understand what it takes to make the entire company work. There will be Craigs who work for you. They will feel entitled to what you have. They may even quit and try to go out on their own. Let them. Once that attitude of entitlement gets too strong, they will become a cancer to the organization. Let them go, but keep the door open for when they fail. Chances are they will not make it, and you may get a new and improved employee back—one whose ego is in check.*

Business Lesson #10... *If someone else can do it better than you, drop your ego and let them. Your chance of success is better. And here is the best part ... you win either way!!*

CHAPTER 6: INCOME COLUMN VS. EXPENSE COLUMN

Business Lesson #11... *It really doesn't matter what your title is or how smart you are. Without sales, you have nothing.*

Business Lesson #12... *People in the revenue (income) column get a certain amount of leeway. (Although we generally don't tell them that.) So, be careful you don't run off your rainmakers with too many silly rules that frustrate them, so they eventually have to take their skill and your revenue to another company.*

CHAPTER 7: IF YOU CAN'T STAND THE HEAT...

Business Lesson #13... *Mentally prepare yourself for the kitchen fires. They will happen, and you probably won't see them coming.*

CHAPTER 8: WHY ARE YOU HERE?

Business Lesson #14... *You better really want this, or you shouldn't do it. Seriously, unless you can't live without it, don't do it.*

CHAPTER 9: CLUELESS TENACITY

Business Lesson #15... *Don't let the mere prospect of having* **NO CLUE** *about what you're doing stop you from pursuing your dreams and ideas. Sometimes you just have to go for it. And then be tenacious about it while you figure it out.*

CHAPTER 10: BUSINESS IS BOTH AN ART AND A SCIENCE

Business Lesson #16... *Answer the "why."*

CHAPTER 11: RUNNING THE NUMBERS—THE SCIENCE

Business Lesson #17... *If you don't have the right kind of data on your business, that is the first thing you need to figure out how to get.*

CHAPTER 12: P&L BY PERSON—OH NO, HERE COMES THE MATH!! AND MORE SCIENCE

Business Lesson #18... *KNOW YOUR NUMBERS. They are your best friends.*

CHAPTER 13: BEING A CEO

Business Lesson #19... *Play the "Would You Rather???" game.*

Business Lesson #20... *Failure isn't the end.* **_IF YOU LEARN,_** *it's the beginning of your next success.*

Business Lesson #21... *Look for the problems and fix them every day — all the time. Always look for what's wrong.*

Business Lesson #22... *Pretending the negative doesn't exist is a recipe for disappointment, depression, and disaster. Understand the deal!!!*

CHAPTER 14: NEGOTIATING—YOU NEED TO BE RELENTLESS

Business Lesson #23... *If you're not good at negotiating, find someone who is.*

Business Lesson #24... *Final thought on walking away. Always remember the winner's curse in negotiating: "Whatever you paid was more than ANYONE else was willing to pay..."*

Business Lesson #25... *The first person to speak after an offer loses. Don't be a loser!!!*

CHAPTER 15: MONEY

Business Lesson #26... *Be careful buying stuff, and remember it's a depreciating asset. The more you buy, the faster it drops in value, and you can never get back what you spent. Your stuff will all eventually be junk anyway.*

Business Lesson #27... *After the bills are paid, safety should be your number one concern before stuff. Stuff should be the reward for the safety net, not the reward for making the money in the first place.*

Business Lesson #28... *Find your passion. Today, it may be paying the bills. Tomorrow, it may be buying things or saving money to give yourself security. But eventually, if you're successful, you will want a legacy. What will yours be?*

Business Lesson #29... *He who* **HOLDS** *the gold rules. When you pay someone, they hold the gold!!*

Business Lesson #30... *Cash is king.*

Business Lesson #31... *Pay yourself. You have no idea what may happen, and if you need it and can't work, you will be glad you have the money.*

CHAPTER 16: TO SELL OR NOT TO SELL

Business Lesson #32... *If you decide to sell, try not to negotiate yourself out of a deal. Be happy with what you get, and don't ever look back. You have no idea what the future holds.*

Business Lesson #33... *If you can make future profits with no risk ... do it.*

Business Lesson #34... *If you're thinking of selling, what are you going to do next?*

CHAPTER 17: BORROWING SOMEONE ELSE'S FILTER

Last Business Lesson #35... *If your filter is not where it should be, find someone who has the experience and the filter to help you get to the next level ... and use them.*

BONUS

Bonus Business Lesson #36... *"Always read to the end of the contract including the fine print—there might be something you miss."*

Bonus Business Lesson #37... *"Don't chase the advice of billionaires. They are so far out of the realm of what you are doing... Their advice probably won't help you. I would rather learn from someone who has succeeded at what I'm doing... Their advice is much more relevant to my daily struggles."*

ABOUT THE AUTHOR

Brian Will is a serial entrepreneur who has created or co-created six very successful companies in four different industries over the last thirty-five years. His first foray into owning his own business was a 10-year stint in the landscaping industry that he started when he was twenty years old. This was followed by three online internet companies during the dot-com boom of the late nineties and early 2000s.

The first was an online health insurance website and call center that was eventually sold to a venture capital company in Silicon Valley and today is one of the largest online Medicare insurance platforms in the US.

The second was an online "lead generation" company in the subprime credit space that was sold to a private equity firm out of Chicago.

The third was another online health insurance website and call center that was sold to another venture capital company in Silicon Valley and today is one of the largest individual state health insurance exchange platforms.

These four exits and the creation of a couple of other companies were followed by several years of consulting projects for both private and public companies in the field of sales and management training.

Although he tried to quit working on multiple occasions, it just wasn't in his nature to sit back and do nothing.

Today Brian owns a growing chain of restaurants in the Atlanta area while he splits his time between the suburbs of Atlanta, Georgia, and Clearwater Beach, Florida.

He is also the very proud father of two adult children.

Having traveled to 25+ countries around the world, Brian considers himself a world-traveler, adventure seeker and adrenaline junkie, but will always be a sucker for a McDonald's coke and some fries.

Made in the USA
Columbia, SC
09 September 2021

45194820R00102